From Feeding Tube to Final Table

A Cancer Survivor's Story

JIM PETZING

Dedication

This book is dedicated to my five angels: Chris F., Elizabeth B., Scott E., Dr. Julie F., and my entire "Circle of Friends" who were there for me when I needed them the most. Thank you for filling me with the strength to keep on fighting.

Contents

Chapter 1
THE FIRST 30 DAYS

HI FRIENDS. I'VE DECIDED TO keep a journal of my journey through the minefield of cancer. This will be a therapeutic way for me to express my thoughts, fears, sadness, and hopefully good news with all of you who are praying for and supporting me during this difficult time. We're going to start at the beginning when I first noticed that something wasn't right. Here's my story:

July 8

I've been in Las Vegas a few days now for the World Series of Poker Main Event. This is my second trip to Vegas this summer. Previously, from May 28 through June 15, I had a great showing with eight cashes in 25 tournaments for total winnings of $27K. I've been feeling really good about my overall poker play this year, and doing quite well, so I decided to play the $10K WSOP Main Event yesterday. Unfortunately I ran into pocket AA, when I had KK, and busted out of the tournament after going all in pre-flop and getting called. I was really disappointed as I had high hopes of getting so much further and ultimately winning the championship for a sweet $8 Million! I guess there's always next year. So today I decided to play in a big tourney at the Venetian. After my shower, I began shaving some scruff off my neck and felt a very large lump on the left side in the lymph node area. It hadn't been there yesterday and seemed quite odd. This lump was hard and had mass, but didn't hurt when I pressed on it. I believed it was an infected lymph node and decided I'd call my doctor and get it looked at when I got home in a week.

July 17

I've been back home now in Douglas, MI for two days. Today I went to see my nurse practitioner in Zeeland. I feel fine, but the lump is still there. It hasn't grown in size. She thinks it might be a bacterial infection in the lymph node and puts me on some high powered antibiotics to knock it out of my system. Pam tells me that if the lump hasn't decreased in size or gone away after the 10 days of meds that I should give her a call. The next step would be to see an ENT (ear, nose throat) doctor. I religiously take the meds and the lump doesn't go away.

July 29

I call Pam today and she gets me an appointment with Dr. Joe Vander-meer, an ENT in Holland, MI.

Aug 1

I arrive at Dr. Vandermeer's office at 6:45am for a 7:10am appointment. They start early on Fridays. I'm concerned about the lump and hope that Dr. V will be able to quickly figure out the problem, give me some new meds, and send me on my way. We chat a bit and I tell him that, along with the lump, my voice has been a bit gravelly, and laryngitis-like for the past four weeks. Next thing I know he numbs my nostrils and puts a long, very thin hose up my nose and down my throat to take pictures. It doesn't hurt. Then he tells me he's going to extract fluid from the lump in my neck and pulls out two syringes. THIS is going to hurt! He inserts each syringe and fills them with fluid from the neck lump. It wasn't that painful. Dr. V tells me that he'll be sending the fluid out for testing. He then shows me the photos from his exploratory of my throat. He notes some swelling on the left side and says that he can't tell what's underneath the swelling quite yet. He seems a bit concerned and, as a poker player, I start to read him. I sense that something isn't right from the look on his face. I ask Dr. V if there's a problem. He's not sure how to respond. I ask him if he thinks I might have cancer. He doesn't want to commit, but gives me the feeling that I may have some type of cancer. He says that we'll know for sure when the test results come back on Monday or Tuesday. My nightmare starts. I've always been a gut person and it's usually right. I leave Dr. V's office knowing that I have cancer, but don't want to believe or accept it. Now I have to wait three or four days to find out for sure. This just can't be. I decide not to say anything to anyone. Yes, this is all a big mistake and everything will be alright. So I go into work at my restaurant, Zing, keep myself busy, hang out with friends, and try not to think about what's really happening. Basically, I put the whole thing "in a box". I've always been good at compartmentalizing, so that's what I did.

Aug 4

It's Monday. I haven't heard anything from Dr. V about my tests. I'm getting anxious. I decide not to call since he did say it might be Tuesday before I hear anything. I get through the day. I can't fall asleep, so I go online to read about neck and throat cancer. This probably wasn't the best idea. I went to the National Cancer Institute site and found that of all cancer cases, only 3-5% are neck cancer. It's quite rare. I then went on to read about the causes (smoking, drinking, HPV virus, etc.), symptoms (some of which I had), repercussions of it, and survival rates. Wish I hadn't done that. I read way more than I should have and learned some things that were quite alarming. The internet certainly has its advantages and disadvantages, but when it comes to cancer it's not filtered or tailored for individual cases. Basically, it outlines a bunch of worst case scenarios. I was really freaked out, so I took a sleeping pill and got a few hours of sleep.

Aug 5

Today the "news" would be coming. I knew in my gut that it wasn't going to be good. I'm probably one of the most positive, optimistic people you will meet, but I wasn't feeling that way at the moment. It was hard to work and I couldn't concentrate. Dr. V had asked me in our August 1 appointment if I wanted to come back in for the results or if a phone call would be okay. I told him I was a big boy and could handle a phone call. It didn't come, so I called his office at 5pm. The woman I spoke with said he was still evaluating the results and would call me before 6pm. He did. The news wasn't good. I had a metastatic squamous cell carcinoma in the left neck lymph node, which meant that the cancer was originating somewhere else and had spread to the neck region. He said that it was imperative that they find the primary cancer site quickly and scheduled me for a laryngoscopy on Thursday. This surgery would allow him to go down my throat with a suspended camera, while under anesthesia, to look for a surface tumor and take biopsies of my tongue, throat and larynx.

It was after this phone call that I think I went into shock. I couldn't believe that I just heard the words, "Yes, Jim, you do have CANCER." WHAT!? Are you kidding me? How could this be? I'm a healthy guy. I've never smoked, don't drink excessively, and am in great shape for my age (53). I have the energy of a 25 year old. And, I DON'T FEEL SICK! I could run a 5K right now, no problem. This can't be right! I got off the phone and started to cry. I was upstairs in the office at the restaurant, so I needed to pull myself together so I could tell Scott, my manager and best friend here in Douglas. He would know something was up with me. I told him. He hugged me. We cried. Scott is one of my angels. I'm going to be depending on him a lot to run my restaurant and be there for me when I get sick. My friend Dave happened to stop by and I decided to tell him. We went downstairs to my martini lounge and had a few drinks. Then we decided to go across the street to The Dunes, our local gay resort, for some more drinks.

What I'm going to tell you now is quite bizarre. While ordering a drink, my friend Mark walked in. He didn't know about my situation since, at this point, I had only told Scott and Dave.

We were chatting at the bar and out of nowhere Mark, for some un-known reason, brought up his previous battle with cancer. I knew he was a cancer survivor, but didn't know his story or the type of cancer he beat. Mark proceeds to tell me that he had battled, of all things, neck cancer! Keep in mind that only 3-5% of all cancers are neck cancer and I live in a tiny town of only 1200 people. How could this be? What are the odds of one of my friends having neck cancer, too?! I said, "Did you have a lump on the side of your neck that was caused by cancer somewhere else in your body and it spread?" He said, "Yes, it originated in my tonsils." I grabbed Mark's hand, took him onto the dance floor and said, "Mark, I just got diagnosed with neck cancer today. Look here! Feel this (pointing to the lump on my neck). The doctors think my primary site is in my throat somewhere." Unfortunately, Mark had waited six months before he had his lump looked at. When they opened him up, he was in late Stage 3 of cancer and they weren't sure they could help him. Ironically, Dr. Joe Vandermeer was his ENT, too. And, Dr. V saved Mark. He's cancer free for six years now! I'm so hopeful. I will beat this, too! Mark assured me that he'd be there for me if I needed him. He said he will tell me what to expect, how I might feel, and what the bad times will be like. I'm feeling somewhat hopeful. He has been through the battle with neck cancer and won! He will be there to guide and support me. Although in shock today, I don't feel so alone. I can do this. Mark beat it. So can I!

Aug 6

I told my friend, Elizabeth, this morning. She works with me at the Saugatuck-Douglas Area Business Association, where I was recruited to be its President after a number of resignations took place about 10 weeks ago. I didn't want to do the job, but because of Elizabeth's passion and energy for wanting to make this community a better place, I decided to give it a go. We've worked hand-in-hand now for 9 weeks and I feel we've already helped make a difference. There's a lot more to do and hopefully I'll be able to continue on while going through my battle with cancer. Elizabeth is another angel. She has a spirituality and goodness that is contagious. Elizabeth is going with me to Holland Hospital today for my Pre-Admission Testing prior to surgery tomorrow. She decides that we're going for a manicure and pedicure on our way to the hospital. So we do. I just love her. The Pre-Admission Test was standard stuff. I'm all registered now for my laryngoscopy/biopsy surgery tomorrow. Elizabeth and I go to Red Dock Cafe to sit outside and take in the beautiful day on the river. The breeze is blowing and I think back to a week earlier when Elizabeth taught me and Chris, my very new boyfriend, how to do stand-up paddle boarding at her local business, Shaka Surf. I hope I'll be able to do that again soon.

Aug 7

It's Thursday, two days since the bomb dropped on me. I've called my family and best friends and told them the horrifying news. Lots of crying. It's still hard for me to believe. Why me? How did I "win" the wrong lottery? It's ridiculous. Those calls were tough, especially my Dad/Stepmom (Cheryl), Brother (Ed), Mom, and Chris. All of my family lives on the East coast in three different states. My mom is 81 and quite arthritic. She feels awful that she can't travel to be with me. I tell her that there's nothing she can do right now and that I'll be fine. She's an awesome woman who has had many of her own battles. She's asking me a lot of questions given her knowledge of science, biology and medicine. Unfortunately, I don't have many answers and won't until my surgery is completed today.

I asked Chris if he would go to the hospital with me. We've only been dating for seven weeks, but are so connected in such a short time. I've been single now for a year and a half and haven't had much luck in the dating scene. I'm a pretty complex guy, often misread and misunderstood, and can be a handful. Chris suddenly came into my life unexpectedly at the right time. I know he's one of my angels, too. He totally gets me and appreciates me for who I am. Chris is very special in so many ways. He's a smart, amazing man, with a big heart and clearly has his priorities straight. He has four beautiful daughters who are his life. I really respect him. Funny how people come in and out of your life. Chris has entered my life for a reason.

We drive my car to Holland Hospital and I'm doing okay. I'm not nervous about the surgery, but rather scared by what they might or might not discover. Dr. V has told me that they need to find the primary site of my cancer so they can figure out the right course of action (surgery, chemo and/or radiation) and get a better handle on my situation. I'm hoping they find it, but also very concerned about what they might find. Has my cancer spread to other places? This is all too surreal. Chris and I get escorted into the pre-op area. He's allowed to be with me, which is great. I get undressed and put on the backless gown. I'm definitely looking "Hot"! Such a fashion statement. We laugh and I get on the bed. It's 10:30am and I'm scheduled for 11:30am surgery. The nurse comes in and takes my vitals, chats with us, and hooks me up to an IV. She is SO nice. I ask her how long she has been a nurse and she says "45 years" with a big smile on her face. We just loved her. Then the waiting began. Dr. V was running late with other surgeries. It was now 12:30pm, one hour after my scheduled surgery time. I was getting anxious and had a mini-meltdown. Just got overwhelmed with everything at that moment. I calmed myself down while Chris sat on my bed holding my hand and touching me sweetly. I gave Chris a list of questions to ask Dr. V during my post-surgery summary. I'd still be knocked out, so I asked Chris to record the conversation with Dr. V if he'd let us. I wanted to be able to send my Dad & Cheryl and Mom exactly what Dr. V actually said in the meeting with Chris, plus I wanted to hear it for myself. Dr. V agreed and Chris did a great job asking all of my questions. He's a TV news producer, so he's good at getting information!

The laryngoscopy/biopsies went well. Dr. V found what he was looking for...a surface tumor at the base of my tongue in the back of my throat near the epiglottis. It was only 1 centimeter in length, so now they have to determine how wide and deep it is under the surface AND if it has spread to any other places. This will be determined by CT scans. I thought I'd feel a lot worse than I did after the laryngoscopy. It wasn't bad at all. Just had a scratchy throat and could only eat soft stuff. When we got back to my place we took a nap and then went to Zing, my restaurant, for dinner. We sat on the garden patio where no one else was dining. Scott, my good friend and restaurant manager, joined us for dinner. I had cream of mushroom soup and crab cakes. Sooooo good! I asked Scott to tell the key people on our staff about my situation, so some of them came out to the patio to give me a hug. It felt good to be with Chris and Scott, and my restaurant family.

Aug 8

It's 12:30am. I just had what felt like a nervous breakdown. I started sobbing out loud and couldn't stop. When I cry, I usually tear up, and don't sob. Chris had fallen asleep and my crying woke him up. I couldn't get Dr. V's voice out of my head telling me I had cancer. It's just something that you don't expect to hear someone say to you. Chris calmed me down and I took another sleeping pill. He fell back asleep and I just laid there in bed looking up at my ceiling fan. I was having a nightmare, right? I'm going to wake up now and everything is going to be alright. Yes, that's what's going to happen. I know it. It's now 2:30am. The pills aren't working. I think about how everyone in town is going to hear about my situation, whether I want them to know or not. It's a lovely place to live, but it's a very gossipy town and rumors abound. I don't want to be a rumor and I don't want to be that person that people whisper about when they come in a room and everyone is looking at them quietly pointing and saying to their friend "Yeah, that's Jim, the owner of Zing. He's the one with CANCER." That would just kill me. I'm way better than a rumor. I'm a fairly public figure in town and many folks know me. I decide that I need to take control of my situation and not be a rumor victim. I go to my Facebook page (James Petzing) and craft a summary of my situation. I hit "Post." There, it's done! Now 860 of my "Friends" know that I have cancer and it's in my own words. It's MY STORY! Did I do the right thing? I hope so. Am I ready for this? What are people going to think, say, do? OMG. I just told the world "I HAVE CANCER!" What? Really? Are you kidding me? Why did I do that? Was I crazy? My gut told me it was the right thing. My gut is usually right. I finally fell asleep.

Friends' Comments:

Tim H.

I've seen you with worse cards than this my friend, and you seem to win the hand. Thanks for sharing and for the tireless energy you've shared with all your friends for so long. We are all here for you in return with support, caring and prayers.

John T.

From the first time I met you I knew you were a power. Then I came to know the extent of what that means. The more I know you the more impressed I am. Amazing is all I can say. Thanks for sharing this. Just know that we are "all in" with you.

Kristin A.

Thank you, Jim, for your courage in sharing your journey. You may never know who all you touch, who you inspire, and who you strengthen through your words. And now it's our job to be YOUR angels. Praying for you, sending strong good vibes your way my friend. You are SO much stronger than any rumor. You control your story (always have!) and we are so fortunate to be hearing it from you. Thank you for your generosity, Jim.

Tina B.

Hey Jim, I'm sorry to hear about your diagnosis. I think you did the right thing in sharing this info. You seem to me like someone who will bear this time in your life better with the support of those who care about you. You'll never be the guy with cancer...not possible. You have way too big a personality and heart for you to ever be minimized to "sick guy." Hang in there and know that healing, caring thoughts are coming your way from Pete and me.

Lee S.

Wow Jim! It is truly amazing how quickly your life can change. It is great to hear that you have such a good network of people around you. Sending positive thoughts your way.

Cheryl C.

Jim, you are surrounded by and supported with such love and positive energy. I am sending mine to you now.

Chris F.

I'm glad I can be here for you. You're a great man... And an excellent writer :)

Mary Kay B.

Mark and I are with you all the way, too. Your energy, positivity and joy of life is infectious and we are praying for your strength along the journey. You have an entire community behind you rooting for your 100% recovery! Lots of love, Mary Kay and Mark

Dan G.

I'm with you every step of the way!

"There is grace in suffering. Suffering is part of the training program for wisdom."

- Ram Dass, "America's Guru"

James P.

We know this has been a tough two weeks. We are with you in our prayers and have you on several prayer lists in our area and in the Northeast. Coming out with your problem is a great move on your part and know that the love of your family and multitude of friends will help to face the CANCER fight that you will conquer. You are dearly loved by Cheryl and me and we will be there for you when you need us. I know your Mom's prayers are with you along with her love. Keep up the fight! You are a winner at everything you have done and you will be a winner this time. Love you so much. Dad and Cheryl

Chapter 2

NOW EVERYONE KNOWS...
AND I'M HAPPY ABOUT THAT!

Aug 8 CONTINUED...

I DIDN'T GET MUCH SLEEP Thursday night, so Friday morning was tough. I decided to embrace Friday like any other. With the shock of the past two days waning a little now, I realized that today was my Dad & Cheryl's anniversary and I had forgot to send a card earlier in the week.

I ran out to the store and got an anniversary card, along with a birthday card for Cheryl (August 12), and sent them "Guaranteed Next Day Delivery" for $19.99. Well that didn't work so well, as the cards arrived on Monday. I'm going to pursue a refund.

I went to work that night a little later than usual. As I was walking to the main entrance of my restaurant, a car drove up and I recognized a nice couple that I know from town. They approached me, gave me a hug and handed me a card. They already knew about my situation.

I was putting it in my pocket to read later when I was alone. Bob (name changed to protect privacy) excitedly said, "No, open it". I did. It had a beautiful handwritten sentiment: "Jim, our thoughts and prayers are with you! We pray this angel will keep you safe and help you get well real soon. Keep this with you at all times. IT WORKS!" Taped to the inside of the card was a beautiful little medallion somewhere between the size of a nickel and a quarter. Gracing it is an angel kneeling in prayer. Bob said to me, "This helped me beat prostate cancer. I carried it into the operating room and held it in my fist even though the surgeons didn't want me to. It works." I hugged Bob, thanked them both, and walked into work with tears in my eyes. This was just the first of many caring gestures to come from folks in my community. I will bring the angel with me to my upcoming doctor appointments.

Aug 9

My "I have cancer" Facebook post generated over 150 caring comments and many new "Friend" requests. I even heard from old high school friends I don't keep in touch with and local people I don't even know. Many shared stories about family members and friends that fought and beat the Big C. Some even knew people with neck cancer. Thoughts and prayers were coming in from everywhere. Folks shared their opinions on the best cancer hospitals to go to and told me I would win this battle against the dirty disease. It felt so good to know that people were there supporting me from near and far. I was energized and ready to take on Saturday night at Zing, which I knew would be busy and full of guests that would want to know more about how I was doing. I was ready to share my situation with those who asked. That night I spent almost an hour chatting with Rick & Jennifer and Brett & Denise. Rick and Brett are dentists and routinely look for tongue cancer in their patients. Brett told me about finding a spot on the tongue of one of his patients. It was cancer and she's being treated now, too. Brett is putting me in touch with her. Then Jennifer told me about Rick's sister. She had kicked cancer's butt and then it came back. She's in treatment now, too, and has written a "tips" booklet for managing cancer. I can't wait to read it. Everyone at the restaurant was so supportive that night. I'm definitely not alone in this battle.

Aug 10

I think I have another lump on the right side of my neck. It's not a large, hard and sturdy lump like the one of the left side of my neck. This one is more like a small floating marble. Am I paranoid now or is my cancer spreading? Please, NO!

Aug 11

I went to Holland Hospital for my CT scan today. This was easy breezy. I got on a long, draped table, fully clothed with sneakers on. That was surprising as I thought I'd have to strip down. Then I was hooked up to an IV and injected with a dye so the scan could pick up any unusual cancer spots. The technician told me that I might experience warmth all over and feel the need to pee. I laughed and then felt my genitals warming up. Hmmm, interesting sensation. I let the technician know that I thought my cancer had spread to the right side of my neck and asked her to please check it. She assured me that the scan would identify a problem , if there was one. I expected the scanner machine to be a coffin-like apparatus. Instead, it was just a large arch that the long table moved back and forth under. I was told by the technician to lie still. Suddenly, I heard the sound of a motor revving up and then out of the blue a recorded voice commanded me to "Breathe in! Hold your breath! Don't move! Relax." Huh, relax? This cycle repeated four or five times. I chuckled to myself. The scans only took 20 minutes. Done. Painless. I asked the technician if she saw any cancer on the right side of my neck. She said, "I can't tell you that." I re-asked the question as, "Was my hypothesis correct?" She replied looking down and away from me meekly saying, "I don't know." We call that a tell in poker. My read on her was that she knew. I think I was right. The cancer was there, too. I so hope I'm wrong.

Aug 12

Today I get to meet my radiation oncologist. Her name is Dr. Julie Forstner and I have been referred to her by Dr. V, my ENT doctor. Dr. Julie is with Metro Health and they are affiliated with the University of Michigan. My appointment was scheduled for 2 1/2 hours and I wasn't sure what to expect as I hadn't really been briefed in advance by Dr. V. I asked Elizabeth if she would go with me to the appointment. I knew I'd be hearing some tough stuff and wanted to be sure someone else processed all the information with me. Elizabeth has been so amazing. After my laryngoscopy last Thursday, I came home to a refrigerator full of three pints of Ben & Jerry ice cream (Half Baked is my favorite), bottled water, and yogurt. So nice.

Elizabeth drove and I asked the male Siri on my IPhone4 for directions. As we made the turn on to Metro Way, we were greeted by a six-story building. There it was, about a quarter mile away. Emblazoned in big bold letters, on the side of the building, was THE CANCER CENTER. We certainly knew we were at the right place. There was no doubt about that. We laughed.

Upon entering, Leslie, the receptionist, greeted us with a warm smile. They were ready for me. I filled out some paperwork, supplied my picture ID (MI Driver's License) and my United Healthcare Insurance Card. By the way, these are asked for at every appointment, along with the exact names and doses of any medication you are taking regularly or even once in a while, including daily vitamins. Additionally, I was asked to complete a form with the names of up to five people who are allowed to get information about/for me from Dr. Julie.

The waiting room felt like a cozy lodge. It was nicely decorated in warm earth tones and comfy chairs and couches. We went to the back and got some water and out came an older woman attached to what appeared

15

to be a chemo drip on a rolling hand cart. I couldn't help but think that, "This will be me in a month or so."

My name was called and we were taken to an examining room. Nurse Rhonda came in and asked me a battery of questions about my general health and the steps of the process I had been through to date, since finding the lump on my neck. We then got to ask her some questions before meeting Dr. Julie. My biggest concern right now is whether I'll be able to talk while undergoing my treatments. Rhonda indicated that I should be able to "whisper", but likely won't want to talk after the radiation and chemo begin to take effect. Sounds like I'm going to have a horribly sore throat for a few months. We finished with Nurse Rhonda and 10 minutes later Dr. Julie Forstner entered the room. Elizabeth and I immediately liked her. Great first impression. She reminded me of my client at Kraft Foods that I worked with for almost ten years when I had my own international marketing training and consulting company. Dr. Julie spent 90 minutes talking with me and Elizabeth about radiation, how it works, what the process will likely be for me, how I'll probably feel, and the benefits of doing radiation along with chemo. Bottom line... It's going to suck! I mentioned that Dr. V and other docs have talked about sending me to the University of Michigan for robotics surgery. She was surprised and thinks that a treatment combination of seven weeks of radiation (Monday through Friday), along with chemo once a week or once every three weeks, will likely be the best course of action. This, she said , will all be dependent upon the results of my biopsies, CT scans and PET scans. So, it's just a "working" plan right now. The good news is that, if I can avoid surgery, there is a high probability that my tongue and neck will be kept intact. Dr. Julie scheduled the PET scans for this Friday. They will be overlaid to the CT scans to make sure that any lymph nodes that may be newly infected with cancer, and aren't picked up by the CT scan, are also identified. Dr. Julie was smart, caring, clear, informational, and down to earth. I hugged her on my way out. I'm so glad that I will be under her care.

TO BE CONTINUED......

Friend's' Comments:

Debbie W.

Jim, thank you so much for sharing your "news" with us at dinner tonight. It makes us both sad but glad you let us know in person about your upcoming journey. Your journal is a great idea for those of us who will want to keep in touch and for you to be able to vent at will! Cancer is ugly. As I mentioned, I know from experience, but the treatments are becoming fine-tuned and more and more "do-able" with help for the side effects improving daily. You are smart, fit and surrounded by people who are pulling for you. Feel those vibes and keep up your winning attitude. You're in our hearts! Debbie and Doug

B J M.

It will "suck", but one day you will wake up and it will be a bad memory that fades with time. Your friends will help you through this and be there to celebrate with you when you are cured!

Mike J.

Glad you decided to start this blog! It's good to be in the know without bombarding you with questions every time I see you. You will be beat this, you're a winner! Glad you've got a doctor you can trust! You are in all of our thoughts and prayers! xo

Paula H.

Jim, I'm so glad you felt a good connection with your doctor and that you've got a good working plan for knocking out that cancer! Continuous prayers for you on your journey.

Dan G.

Sweet Jim, I think you are a brave soldier and will begin the battle with fortitude and grace. Your updates are full of descriptive detail and your willingness to open up and share is brave and generous. Love you and my prayers and thoughts are with you 24/7.

Chapter 3

Feeling Frustrated...I Just Want to Get My Treatment Started

Aug 13

Even given the bad situation I'm in, I felt really good after my meeting with Dr. Julie yesterday. It will be awesome if I can avoid invasive surgery, but need to keep the option open if that's what the experts recommend down the road. It was nice not having any "cancer" appointments today. I needed a break from it. I started the day at 8:30am with our monthly Saugatuck-Douglas Area Business Association meeting. Sadly, only five folks attended it, along with me (the Interim President filling a seven-month term as a result of the resignations of the previous two Co-Presidents), Elizabeth (our Marketing and Member Services Manager...and one of my angels), our summer intern, Maddie (we will miss her a lot when she goes back to school), and six of our Board members. This is a typical turnout, especially during the summer months when our membership is crazy busy (and exhausted from) trying to maximize their sales during a very short 10 to 12 week seasonal window. Additionally, the previous image of the Business Association hasn't been stellar and most members don't think much of the organization, so I'm working hard with Elizabeth and the Board to turn that around. We've made tons of progress and achieved some significant wins during my nine-week tenure so far. However, when I was voted by the Board to take on the position, there was not a set of officers in place and to date we still don't have one. My upcoming battle with cancer could pose a greater problem, so I felt it was very important that we get a Vice President and Secretary in place now (we already have a Treasurer). Then, when I start feeling really sick in mid-October, the Vice President can temporarily take the helm until I'm back on my feet.

Elizabeth and I decided to let the Board know about my situation (I had already Facebook'd it, so some knew) and we asked for volunteers to take on the role of VP and Secretary. You could hear "crickets in the room." I was really disappointed that no one said "Hey Jim, I'd love to do it until you're back in action...I'm up for the challenge." Elizabeth and I looked at each other and rolled our eyes. Finally, one of the Board members said she'd be a Co-Vice President if someone else would do it with her. Another Board member agreed to do the same, so that's how we're going to manage through the winter months while I'm healing and getting better. Of course, no one wanted to be Secretary and take notes at every meeting, so we'll have to try to find another intern and give that responsibility to them. Or, I guess Elizabeth will have to do that, too. She's already doing so much. I hope we can find some new Board members soon that will step up and be leaders. This organization has so much potential. I'm really bummed that I'm going to be incapacitated for a while and not be able to move things forward as quickly as I want. I have so many ideas to help the businesses in our community build their respective businesses, but there's just so much apathy. It's sad that very few people want to roll up their sleeves, get dirty, and invest the time and energy necessary to get us to the next level. It's so frustrating!

Aug 14

I was really excited for today because I would be meeting with Dr. V to get my tissue biopsy and CT scan results. Well, things didn't go as planned. Dr. V was on vacation with his family, so I met with his uncle, Dr. Peter Vandermeer. Chris came with me. I've decided that I want one of my angels (Elizabeth, Chris or Scott) to always be by my side when information is being shared by one of the doctors. There is a lot to process in these sessions. I want to be sure that I understand everything being said so I can explain it to my family when they call each night to get updates on my doctor visits. Sometimes I have what I'm calling "detached moments", when I hear or learn something that concerns or scares me regarding the potential treatments and/or possible outcomes. I kind of go into a daze and then force myself to snap out of it. I have to know everything I can about what I'll be up against, so I can make an informed decision about my treatment plan when it comes time to do that in the next few weeks. Chris is a great listener and processor of information. He works in the "news" field, so he is skilled at fact collecting, connecting the pieces, and asking the right questions. Together, we're a good team. Dr. Peter V spent over an hour with us, but did not have my tissue biopsy results. He told me Holland Hospital sent them to the Mayo Clinic for evaluation. I didn't know if that was a good or bad thing, so I asked him. Dr. Peter V said that it's common practice when there are inconsistencies, irregularities, inconclusive findings, or questions with the test. It's a big piece of the puzzle that we need to have in place before I can have my consult with Dr. Prince, the surgeon at University of Michigan who I'll be meeting with on September 4. Dr. Peter told me that we may not hear anything for ten days to two weeks from when the Mayo Clinic received the tissue biopsies from Holland Hospital. It's Day 7 now. Hopefully they'll be in by this coming Tuesday when I meet again with Dr. Julie, my radiology oncologist.

I then inquired about my CT scan results from Monday. As I thought, the cancer has spread to the right side of my neck. I had felt that "floater", about the size of a pea, back inside the middle of my right neck when I pushed on it last Sunday. Dr. Peter V indicated that they actually saw a total of three, and possibly four, lymph nodes already infected with the cancer. Great, the cancer is spreading! Lucky me...I'm one of the 40% of neck cancer victims whose cancer spreads from one side to the other. I'm told it's because of the location of my primary cancer site on the bottom left side of the tongue at the back of my throat near the epiglottis. It is somehow connected to the lymphatic system, which feeds both sides of the neck and throat. I feel like I just had a "bad beat" at the poker table... again. On the positive side, as long as my cancer spreads and stays in the neck and throat region, it is more easily treatable. If it travels up or down from there, I'm going to have an even bigger problem. Dr. Peter V was generous with his time, informative, and answered all of our questions to the best of his ability, even with the missing puzzle pieces (tissue biopsies and PET scan, which is scheduled for tomorrow). He thinks the lump on the left side of my neck (4 1/2 centimeters) may not react well to radiation and chemo because he surmises that many of the matted lymph nodes are fully developed, "hibernating", and aren't hungry or active. Generally, radiation and chemo works best with "hungry" types of cells and not the hibernating, more inactive kind. This is a different perspective than Dr. Julie currently has right now. Dr. Peter V also thinks that the primary site tumor will likely need to be removed surgically via a robotic arm because it's in such a hard to reach, small area. NOOOO! I was so hoping that invasive surgery wouldn't have to be part of the treatment plan. If it is, there will have to be a determination made of whether it's surgery first followed by radiation and chemo or vice versa. Now I'm frustrated and a little confused, but am told by Dr. Peter V that it's common for different doctors in different cancer specialties to have different opinions and points of view. I get that. It's just frustrating. I want there to be consistency in what people think, say, and recommend. It will help me determine what I should do and agree to for my treatment.

Before we wrapped up, I asked Dr. Peter V the following question: "If you were me and in this situation, what would you choose as your course of treatment?" Without having all the pieces in place yet, he said he would first start with intensive radiation and chemo and hope that it quickly shrinks down the lump on the left side of my neck, along with the other infected lymph nodes throughout the neck region. If the left side lump doesn't shrink in size during the first few weeks, it's probably full of those hibernating cancer-ridden lymph nodes that will have to be surgically removed. So, at this point, it looks like there's a good chance that my ultimate treatment will be a combination of radiation, chemo and surgery. We'll see what Dr. Julie thinks on Tuesday. I went back to work that afternoon and couldn't really concentrate. A couple of my staff members asked how my appointment went and I told them what I've written here.

Now I'm really frustrated. I just want to get my treatments going. My cancer is spreading and I am waiting for things that are out of my control. That's really hard for me as I'm a bit of a control freak, very organized, and always have a plan built to achieve a goal...plus a back-up plan if that doesn't work. But, not this time. Now I'm in what I call my "black hole phase"... floundering around aimlessly with no specific direction or clear destination. I'm living in a world of gray, when I'm a black and white kind of guy. I just want to get moving. I don't want to waste any time. I'm getting impatient. My mother always reminded me as a kid that "patience is a virtue". Guess I need to remind myself of that, let the experts do their thing, hold on tight, and believe that waiting will result in a better, more informed course of action and treatment plan. I can do this, but it's not easy. Waiting for the answers is so frustrating.

TO BE CONTINUED....

Friends' Comments:

Karen/Mike Z

Ahhhh...yes. Patience. In my opinion, one of the hardest virtues! "God, give me patience...now!" The waiting game is tough, but you are most definitely tougher and stronger. Find peace within all of this chaos and you will find even more inner-strength to get you through this anxi-

Jim Petzing

ety-ridden waiting period. Continued prayers and positive thoughts here are sent your way!!

BJM

This is a high wire. One -- always question and push for more, quicker action, if you think it is necessary. Two -- respect the doctors and figure out when you need to be patient. If you fall the wrong way, get right back up and move in the right direction. Listen to your gut. You've got what it takes.

Mary Kay B.

Praying for patience and wisdom for the best course of treatment. Thankful that your angels are with you at each appointment.

Elizabeth B.

My darling Jim- You are an inspiration to those of us who are alongside you on this challenging health journey. When you are frustrated with the waiting, know that we share in the frustration and long to ease your mind! Tuesday will be here before you know it. We'll hit the drive-thru at Starbucks and head to Dr. Julie's digs. Cake pops all around! Her smiling face and calming demeanor will bring you some well-deserved peace of mind. Our thoughts are our reality - positivity is the name of the game here! I am available 24/7 to lend an ear, bring some ice cream, road trip to our billboard (just to see it lit up at night!) or watch Netflix! So many choices. One thing is constant..the love and well wishes of those who love and care for you will surround you and lift you up when you cannot get there alone! We share the joys and pains alongside you, spreading the burden makes the load lighter. So, the more you share, the more we can help lighten the load. Love you sweetheart - Big smooch coming your way;) xoxoxo

24

Chapter 4

Can't Move Forward Without ALL the Pieces to the Puzzle!

Aug 15

I HAD A LOT OF work to do and emails to respond to yesterday when I got back to Zing after the appointment with Dr. Peter V. Learning that the tissue biopsy results from Mayo Clinic weren't in yet and that surgery was now likely going to be part of my treatment plan came as a bit of a blow. I couldn't concentrate. By the time 6pm rolled around, I knew I wasn't in an appropriate state of mind to be on the floor for dinner, so I went home emotionally drained and teary-eyed. After pulling myself together, I called my Mom and Cheryl, my stepmom, to fill them in on the latest news that my cancer had spread from the left side to the right side of my neck and that the biopsies were missing in action. I was wound up from the day, so took a sleeping pill and fell asleep around 1:30am. My iPhone4 alarm awakened me at 6:15am. I quickly showered, dressed, and got in the car for my 40 minute ride to Metro Health Hospital in Wyoming, MI (near Grand Rapids), across the street from The Cancer Center, where Dr. Julie, my radiology oncologist, has her office.

It was PET scan day. Dr. Julie had set this up for me to find the cancer "hot spots" that the CT scan I had on Monday might not have picked up. She called it an "insurance policy" for making sure that all the newly developing and smaller active cancer cells are identified, along with any "at risk" cells. I parked in the lot outside the Emergency Room entrance and followed a very pregnant woman and her man into the check-in area. She was in labor and her contractions were six minutes apart. I couldn't help but think, "Wow, she's going to bring a new life into this world in just a few minutes or hours. And I'm here trying to save my life after 53 years of living." It was a bizarre moment. I was told by the receptionist that I went in the wrong door and was directed down a long, carpeted hallway to the main lobby for registration.

Ironically, a World Poker Tour event was on the television in the waiting room. For those of you that don't know it, I'm a world ranked professional poker player in my eighth year of competitive tournament play. I had an amazing summer playing in Vegas for 18 days from May 28-June 15. I grossed $27K, including min cashing in two World Series of Poker events and a final table 6th place finish in a Venetian DeepStack event for $19K. I went back to Vegas on July 6 to play the $10K Main Event on July 7 where I was knocked out during late Day 1 with my KK vs AA all-in pre-flop. It was the start of what we call a "bad run" in poker. The next day I found the lump on my neck and I busted out of another tourney with KK vs AA all in pre-flop. The odds of that happening in back-to-back tourneys are ridiculously low, but it happened to me. And then, to top it all off, I "goose-egged" the entire week by not cashing in any tournaments.

The PET scan was pretty simple. I wasn't allowed to eat any carbs, sweets, fruits, or caffeine for the previous 12 hours. The female technician searched for a vein to take some blood for a blood sugar test. Fortunately, I have great veins for blood work and have had many tests over my almost 54 years. I've even been complimented on my veins because they are so present. But no, she went for the one vein that you can barely see on the underside of my lower left arm and missed it big time! I jumped and yelled out "Ouch, what are you doing?!" I was bleeding a lot. She apologized saying "Sorry, I should have gone for the other one". No kidding. She clearly wasn't awake yet at 8am. I scored an 89, which she proclaimed was good. They then made me drink a large, very sweet, Strawberry Kiwi drink from a straw. It was like Kool-Aid, which I never was a fan of as a kid. Any "hungry" cancer cells in my body will be eager to enjoy this sugar infusion. Then they'll "glow" during the scan.

After waiting 75 minutes for the sugar to get into my system, I was taken to the portable PET scan mobile that was very professional looking and attached to the hospital wing I was in. I learned later that that it's a VERY expensive piece of equipment ($1.5-$2MM) that hospitals can't afford to have on their own. This one travels the area's hospital circuit doing eight or so scans a day. The machine was quite large with a long-padded table extending vertically from the center of what looked a big bagel with a hole in the middle. I got on the "bed" fully clothed and dozed a bit during the 35 minutes of scans, while I moved back and forth through the center of the "bagel". This was easy breezy, too, just like the CT scan. They said Dr. Julie would have the results on Monday, in time for our Tuesday meeting. This would complete the second piece of the trifecta puzzle. We'd be in great shape now to move forward, if the Mayo Clinic could just get my doctors the tissue biopsy results.

Aug 16 & 17

So much love and support coming to me via Facebook, this site (CaringBridge.org, where I'm keeping my blog), and my restaurant customers, along with calls from family and friends. I feel like the Saugatuck-Douglas community is reaching out and giving me a big hug. It feels good. I'm so glad I publicly "outed" my status on Facebook and have freely talked about my situation. I'm excited to contact my 1-on-1 cancer mentor from Imerman Angels. He's 55, lives in IL and has been through his own battle with neck cancer. I'll contact him after Tuesday's meeting with Dr. Julie, once all the pieces of the puzzle are in. He has already called and left a voice mail message. I'm hoping he can be a coach and role model for me.

TO BE CONTINUED....

Friends' Comments:

Lauren F.
Sending you love, Jim!

Duane M.
Just know there is a ton of love, prayers and support for you, Jim. Stay strong and positive. You will be holding the AA winning hand at the end of this!

Chapter 5

Hoping for Some Good News,
Preparing for the Worst

Aug 18

I'm on pins and needles praying that the PET scans don't show the cancer spreading to other parts of my body. If it stays localized in the neck region, I have a much better chance for success with the treatments. I'm also hoping that the Mayo Clinic has finished their evaluation of my tissue biopsies and delivered their findings to both Dr. V, my ENT, and Dr. Julie, my radiation oncologist. If these final two pieces of the puzzle are completed, I will receive a recommended course of action from Dr. Julie during our scheduled appointment tomorrow.

At 4pm, my cell phone rang and I saw it was Dr. Julie's office calling. It was the receptionist and she told me that Dr. Julie wanted to move our appointment up from 2:30pm to 2pm. When I asked her "Why?", she said: "Dr. Julie would like to have more time with you to review the results of your PET scans." This couldn't be good. Have you ever had a doctor's office call and tell you they want to spend MORE time with you during your appointment? I've never heard of that happening and became quite concerned. I thought to myself, "If everything was status quo and just reinforced the CT scan findings, then why would she need more time with me? Did the tissue biopsies come in and show that the cancer was spreading outside of the neck region and into my chest, throat, lungs, pancreas, brain or somewhere else?" I was very concerned about the receptionist's request and started thinking about worst case scenarios. NO....please don't tell me that this nightmare is going to be worse than it already is! Can someone wake me up now? This unusual phone call was making me crazy with paranoia. I couldn't concentrate or work, so I stayed upstairs in my office and called friends, checked emails, looked at Facebook, and tried to take my mind off this disturbing situation. Michelle, a good friend and tenant in my apartment above Zing, saw the light on in my office at about midnight, came upstairs, knocked on the door, and wanted to chat. She hadn't really acknowledged my cancer diagnosis until this moment. Michelle told me that her Mom had died from cancer three years ago, and that she, Michelle, found it extremely difficult to engage in conversations about cancer, especially with a bestie. We've known each other for a little over two years and have grown close. Michelle was pained by my cancer diagnosis and wanted to know how I was doing. She invited me over to her place for drinks. After a couple of Bombay Gins on the rocks, I made my way home at 2am and was awake until 4am when my sleeping pill finally kicked in. I was so worried about what I might learn tomorrow and started mentally preparing for the worst.

Aug 19

It's 1am Eastern time now (Aug 20). What a day I've had. My appointment with Dr. Julie could not have gone better. I've got GREAT NEWS! 1) The tissue biopsy and PET scan results were both in and showed that my cancer has not spread outside of the neck region. I am so relieved. You have no idea! 2) Dr. Julie's course of action does not include invasive surgery at this time. In fact, she gave me 80/20 odds that I will not need surgery at all. She believes that a combination of intensive radiation and chemotherapy should be able to kill off the cancer in both the left and right side of my neck, and bilaterally along the base tongue at the top of my throat near the epiglottis. Dr. Julie will consult tomorrow with her boss, the world renown expert of head and neck radiology at the University of Michigan Medical Hospital in Ann Arbor. He will review my case and work with her to develop the right radiation plan. Dr. Julie will also be setting me up with the chemotherapy group at The Cancer Center. 3) I will start my treatment program on Tuesday, September 2, the day after Labor Day. This is three weeks earlier than I anticipated and is a great thing as my cancer is definitely growing on both sides of my neck.

Dr. Julie doesn't want to wait and neither do I! All of my treatments will be conducted at The Cancer Center in Wyoming, MI about 35-40 minutes from my hometown of Douglas, MI. I will be going to radiation daily and chemotherapy weekly for a total of seven weeks, wrapping up treatments around October 21st.

I know it's going to be a tough road, but I've got this! My angel, Elizabeth, was with me today. She was by my side for this good news! She even bought a gift from us for Dr. Julie, a bag of Colombian coffee beans. We loved Dr. Julie after our first meeting last Tuesday and love her even more now! Dr. Julie is my fourth angel. She joins Elizabeth, Scott, and Chris. We did a group hug on the way out of her office. I also carried the "praying angel" medallion that was given to me last week by a sweet local couple. I kept it in my left hand during the appointment today. I know it helped protect me from bad news. When Elizabeth and I walked out the door of The Cancer Center, we did a happy dance. Yes, I have the big, nasty C, but it didn't spread. Thankfully, I don't need surgery (right now and hopefully not ever), and the waiting is over! I have an action plan and I'm ready to get started.

After Elizabeth dropped me off at Zing, she headed to Holland to run some errands. We had torrential downpours and rain showers throughout the day, but now the sun had broken through the clouds. I received a text from Elizabeth. She said, "This is for you." It was a beautiful picture of a rainbow that she had just photographed. At the end of that rainbow is "Cancer-FREE me." I just know it!

Friends' Comments:

Paula H.
JOY, JOY, JOY! So wonderful to get this happy news!!

Debbie W.
Hey Jim, I'm reading this through tears of JOY! Your posts have been amazing and I am so, so relieved and thrilled for you. Onward and upward! Debbie and Doug

Duane M.
AWESOME NEWS! You drew the pair of Aces and you are all in. Knock the "C" off the table, Jim! Prayers continue.

Tim H.
Wow!! This is awesome news. Way to go Jim and way to make things happen for the positive. Your body is responding to the conviction and support of you and your team. Happy dance is right!

John T.
What Jim did not mention was that after his busy day he showed up for a 5:30 meeting in downtown Douglas to help our business group plan for the future and meet our challenges. What a guy!

Jim's Rainbow!
Journal entry by Elizabeth B. (8/20/2014)

Here is that beautiful rainbow I saw today after learning the wonderful news about your excellent prognosis! I do not believe in coincidence, but rather a tangible sign and God's promise that you will crush this cancer. I smiled as I snapped the picture of a rainbow that literally appeared directly in front of me after a day of torrential rains and gloomy skies. You, my friend, will help others as you battle this disease and our higher power recognizes the beauty within you. Your journal entries have touched all of us. I am awake at 4am full of gratitude for the great news we heard yesterday! Grateful for your friendship and God's never ending LOVE. So happy for you and the rest of us who get to support and love you through treatment.

Jim P.
"Cancer-FREE Me" is at the end of this rainbow. That will be my pot of gold! Thanks for posting this, Elizabeth.

Chapter 6

On Cloud 9 (Relatively Speaking)

Aug 20

I can't begin to tell you the overwhelming relief I had after Elizabeth and I heard the great news yesterday about my cancer not spreading above or below the neck region, where it currently has made its temporary home. Little does this unruly tenant know, but I'm working on an eviction order. I've had a day now to process the positive headline news of yesterday and so wanted to shout it aloud for the whole world to hear. I'm feeling like I just won $1MM and am beyond grateful. The emotional release felt so good when I sobbed on Elizabeth's shoulder in her car after our appointment with Dr. Julie at The Cancer Center. The happy tears kept flowing when I called Chris, another one of my angels and the special guy in my life, on our car ride back home.

What was a very gray and horribly rainy day just turned into a sunshiny day, both literally and figuratively. I was on Cloud 9 and had a new pep in my step. It was like the weight of the world had been lifted off of my shoulders. I could breathe easier again. I was re-invigorated! I found it ironic that even with all of the fabulous news of yesterday, I still am riddled with cancer and have a tough battle ahead of me. I've realized that "great news" takes on different meanings depending on your own personal situation. It's all relative.

Today was "Dentist Day". Given that I'll be receiving intensive radiation in my neck and throat area daily for seven weeks, my mouth will be totally exposed and is at risk of being negatively affected if all is not well with my teeth and gums. So one of the pre-radiation requirements is passing an extensive dental examination. I drove 40 miles to Kentwood, MI to meet with Dr. Scott. He was recommended by Dr. Julie. I was there for almost two hours. His team took x-rays of every tooth, checked my gums, fillings, and crowns, and evaluated me for overall oral health. I passed with flying colors. Dr. Scott said that he hadn't had anyone in his chair for a very long time that didn't need something fixed prior to radiation. I was thankful that my Mom was diligent about my dental and orthodontic care while growing up. I carried that practice with me into adulthood and now it's paying dividends.

After the dental exam, I drove back to the office to meet with Scott, my manager at Zing. We had so much to catch up on after his recent week of vacation and decided to have a mid-day breakfast on our front patio at the restaurant. Scott is a great friend, one of my angels, and takes care of Zing like it's his own baby. I'm not worried too much about Zing while I go through treatments. I know Scott will do a super job running the show, which he'll tell you he does already anyway. He lets me think I'm in charge, but he's really the Wizard of Zing.

After another local appointment, I drove back to Kentwood to Dr. Scott's office for an intensive teeth cleaning. It took about an hour and then I was back on the road again to Douglas. Wow, 160 miles today for the dentist. I listened to the Van 92.7 and heard the radio spot I wrote and recorded for Sidewalk Sale Day. I taped it in my used car salesman voice. It's definitely reminiscent of one of those deep, deep discount ads you see on TV and roll your eyes at. But it breaks through the clutter and does grab your attention, so I'm happy with it.

I was ready to do something fun, so after chatting with local Rotary folks who had a Happy Hour social at Zing, I went over to the Dunes Resort for Drag Bingo and a barbecue. I met Scott and some other friends there. We drank, ate, lost money and had a fun time. My friend Mike (who I play poker with) and his girlfriend, Kris, invited all of us out on their new pontoon boat. We drove five minutes over to Saugatuck, hopped on, and headed down the river. Mike had an amazing music mix. We drank, chatted, danced and watched a stunning sunset over the lake. I didn't want to go at first because I was so exhausted from lack of sleep the past few nights and the busy day of driving and appointments, but I'm so glad that I did. I had a blast! It was just what I needed.

I got home and watched the end of America's Got Talent (The Results show). Then I decided to call Tammy, a tongue cancer survivor. She is the patient of a dentist, Brett, that comes to my restaurant a lot. Brett found her cancer spot when doing a routine check of her mouth and tongue during a teeth cleaning. I hope all of your dentists are doing that each time you see them. Brett called Tammy on my behalf and asked her if she would be open to talking with me about her journey and battle with cancer. We spoke for almost an hour. I learned a lot. She knows Dr. Julie's boss, Dr. Avi, at University of Michigan, and a number of surgeons there. I told her that Dr. Julie doesn't think I should start with surgery and that I likely won't need it. Tammy highly encouraged me to keep my consult appointment with the neck cancer surgeon, Dr. Prince, at the University of Michigan on September 4. She thinks it's important I hear from him directly that surgery should not be the first thing I do before I begin my radiation and chemo treatments. I think I might call Dr. Julie today and move my start date back a week from September 2 to September 9, just to be sure. Tammy was so generous with her time and counsel. I really liked her and look forward to keeping in touch. Overall, it has been a good past two days. I'm exhausted and ready for bed. I need the sleep.

Aug 21

Today is my birthday. I'm 54 and have cancer. Wow, didn't expect to be saying that! I got the best birthday gift ever on Tuesday when I found out that my cancer isn't spreading beyond the neck region into other parts of my body. It's still hard for me to grasp, but I'm dealing with all of this as positively as I can. Birthdays are supposed to be happy celebrations of our birth, life and all the good things that lie ahead because with birth comes life. Now I'm in the fight for my life!

I have to admit that death is crossing my mind today. I can't help it. I have cancer. It's like I have an angel on one shoulder and a devil on the other. The angel is saying: "You've got this! You will beat the nasty C because you are a fighter and a winner." The devil is saying: "Don't be so sure. I'm there until you get rid of me. I'm lurking. I'm lethal. Watch out, I'm coming to get you." I try to ignore the devil and only listen to the angel. They're fighting with each other. I hope the angel and I beat that devil bastard. We just can't lose. It's not in the cards. I'm too good of a player. I usually win at everything I do. Is this my time to lose? No, it can't be. It doesn't make any sense. ARGH. The Life and Death balance is so fragile. Okay, enough of this back and forth. It's My Birthday and I'm going to have fun tonight with my friends at Marro's (my fave Italian restaurant in Saugatuck) and then karaoke at the Dunes afterwards. Yes, I will be singing some of my standard favorites while I still can: Downtown, Forever in Blue Jeans, Sweet Caroline, 9 to 5, Copacabana, and The Candy Man. Looking forward to this evening after I go check on Sidewalk Sale Day in Douglas and work at our Saugatuck-Douglas Area Business Association booth in Saugatuck later this afternoon.

Friends' Comments:

Kat T.
You write so well, Jim! I think this "hurdle" may have been put there to encourage your eloquent and humorous style. Keep up the journaling! Love to you and all your angels.

Duane M.
Happy B-Day! Live life to the fullest. Thank you for keeping us posted on the journey. Keep smiling (it will show off those clean teeth) Carpe Diem!

Chapter 7

I've Been Given A Gift?

Aug 22

I HAD A VERY NICE birthday yesterday. It was low key and just what I needed. Scott pulled together a small gathering of friends that met us at The Dunes after dinner for karaoke. The boys had decorated the cabaret with helium balloons, so it looked quite festive. Scott arranged to have colorfully decorated cupcakes brought out and, of course, the Happy Birthday song was sung. Many folks on my Zing staff came by and I really appreciated that!

I received a thought-provoking Facebook message from an acquaintance the other day that really made me think and take a step back for a moment. She's a cancer survivor and in it she says: "Once you are through all of this, you will be so much more appreciative of everything, big and small, in your life. You will be more positive and happy. You know what it's like to look down the barrel now. You will then need to lend your support and give reassurance to those who will be staring down that barrel. You've been given a gift that will enrich your life. You will see."

How could this horrible, debilitating disease of cancer be a gift? As I processed this more, I saw the silver lining she was referring to. Perhaps, at some point, I'll be able to help others in a way that I don't even realize yet? Maybe the Big C really is a gift and I'm supposed to benefit others down the road through my experience? I will embrace this thought as I move into battle.

Aug 23

I called Dr. Julie's office yesterday to discuss whether she had spoken yet with her boss, Dr. Ari, the world renown radiation oncologist at University of Michigan, and to see if she had made contact yet with Dr. Prince, the surgeon who was assigned to my case. I'm really struggling with the order that my treatment should take. Should it be a combo of radiation/chemo first with the hope that it kills off all the cancer, as Dr. Julie recommends. Or, should it be surgery followed by radiation/chemo as others have suggested? Dr. Julie responded quickly to my call and we had a good chat. She had spoken with Dr. Ari, who agreed with her position on the treatment plan. Dr. Julie also connected with Dr. Joe Vandermeer who did my laryngoscopy. It appears that he's also on board with the radiation/chemo approach first, followed by surgery if it doesn't crush the cancer.

I asked Dr. Julie to please contact Dr. Prince, who she has worked with before, and run my case by him to get his surgical opinion. Dr. Julie said she would and that she'd get back to me early next week. I really trust her. Whether I have surgery or not, I'm going to need radiation/chemo so I know that she's being objective and wants what's best for me. I'm anxious to see what Dr. Prince says and I may ask to speak with him by phone next week.

Today, Chris and I are heading to Long Beach, IN, part of Michigan City, IN, to my good friend Tim's beach house. Many of my best Chicago friends will be there. I haven't seen most of them since our annual Christmas brunch. I'm excited to see them, while having them see me looking healthy before I start my treatments after Labor Day. I wonder how they're going to react to me? Only a few have reached out since I got my cancer diagnosis. I'm sure it's a little awkward since I don't see them regularly anymore. Regardless, we're going to have a great time! It's one of the last times I'll be able to let loose, have a few drinks, and be silly before the radiation and chemo take effect. I'm glad Chris is coming with me.

We're getting very close to each other. I want him to meet the guys I hung out with over the past ten years, including my ex-partner, Matt.

TO BE CONTINUED....

Friends' Comments:

Jeanne S.
Jim, you will find that some friends will be with you for better and for worse, and some of your friends will not be able to reach out to you as they are afraid they "won't say or do the right things", but please know that they are always thinking of you. My sister experienced that and I was the middle man in some instances. She would say to me "but I haven't changed." Unfortunately, there are some people that just can't handle the Big C. It's important to always have that glass half-full attitude. Always. That will get you through your tough battle ahead. Stay strong!

Chapter 8

Helping Me, Helping You

Aug 24

I ENJOYED MY OVERNIGHT TRIP with Chris to see my Chicago friends at Tim's beach house in Michigan City (Long Beach), IN. There were 11 of us. It's the first time I'd seen most of the guys as a group since our annual Christmas brunch back in December. We drank, told stories that can't be repeated, ate brats, dogs, mac n cheese and some cold salads for dinner, and took in a beautiful sunset over Lake Michigan. Chris fit right in. It was a relaxing getaway. However, I have to admit that I was a bit disappointed that a couple of my "best" friends didn't pull me aside to have a one-on-one chat about how I've been doing with all the cancer stuff. We talked about it briefly as a group, but not individually. I guess I expected more empathy or at least a more personal check in with me. Perhaps they just don't know how to respond to a good friend with cancer? We'll see what happens as things get more difficult for me. Chris and I got back to my place late this afternoon and went to see Beehive, a musical at the Saugatuck Center for the Arts, with Elizabeth and Scott. It was a Broadway caliber show featuring six talented women, singing, dancing, and taking us through the advancement of women, fashion, and music during the 1960s.. Beehive was so much fun! It took my mind off of everything for a couple of hours. And it was nice being there with three of my angels.

Aug 25

I received a note on Facebook Messenger last Friday that has really hit a chord with me. It was from a friend, Andrew (name changed to protect privacy), that used to live here in Douglas. We went out socially a few times and often saw each other at the Dunes Resort pool and bar. Andrew's note validated for me how my journal entries are not only helping me therapeutically, but also are helping others.

He wrote the following: "Jim, I just want to thank you for being amazing, brave and strong in sharing your experience. Cancer is VERY prevalent in my family and I know it's very likely something that I'll have to deal with. My family tends to be secretive about these sorts of things. But you sharing your experience, and especially your feelings, is so touching and helpful to me. I have always feared that unknown experience that I will likely face. You making it more known to me has given me some calm and control of my own fears. You are amazing and I am grateful for the lessons you are teaching me each day."

Andrew's note made MY day. I was so excited that I was having a positive impact on him. I responded back to him saying: "Andrew, thanks so much for your nice note. I'm glad my journal is helping you. I struggled with how personal to get in it, but decided to go for it with the hope it would make a difference for folks along the way, while being therapeutic for me. I start radiation/chemo next Tuesday and am anxious about it, but ready. Thanks for letting me know that my journal is having a positive impact on you!" I'm so hoping that it's having a similar impact on others, too.

Today I met my chemo doctor, Dr. Zachem. He and his staff are also located in The Cancer Center, along with Dr. Julie, my radiation oncologist. Chris accompanied me for moral support. I was there for three hours. I started with Kendra who updated my medical history, weighed me in at 226.7 lbs clothed, and took my vitals. Then I had blood taken at the lab to serve as a baseline as we move forward with the chemo. Dr. Zachem came in and spent a good 45 minutes with me and Chris. He explained the weekly chemo process, how it will work on fighting my cancer in tandem with the seven weeks of daily radiation treatments, and what I can expect as side effects, including the possibility of needing a feeding tube since my throat likely will be unbearably sore.

I liked Dr. Zachem. He also encouraged me to keep my September 4 consult with Dr. Prince, the surgeon assigned to me at University of Michigan medical hospital, if we have to go that route at some point. I will drive to Ann Arbor with Scott early next Thursday morning to see Dr. Prince. Dr. Zachem decided that Tuesdays will be my combined radiation/chemo day and that I'll need to allow four hours for treatments on those days. So, Tuesday, September 2 will be my first day of treatment and include both radiation and chemo. FUN! My radiation appointments are at 3:10pm at The Cancer Center for the remainder of that week, so I can still get my treatment after my consult with Dr. Prince from 9am to 12noon on Thursday.

Along with Dr. Zachem and Kendra, I met with a number of his team members including, Rita, the patient navigator, Jen, the chemo nurse, and Tracy, the social worker. I haven't met the dietician yet, but likely will on Tuesday. I liked everyone a lot! They were open, honest, informative and straight-shooting. I feel like the whole is greater than the sum of its parts and that I'll be in good hands with this team. I knew I was in the right place when Rita out of the blue said: " I would trust Dr, Zachem with my own life. He truly is amazing." I can't even begin to tell you how reassuring it was to hear that incredible testimonial from Rita. Her job is to coordinate with everyone on my behalf and be my primary point person. In a way, she's like an in-house patient advocate. I like the concept a lot and know she'll be helpful to me.

It was an emotional chemo orientation. I learned that I will be treated very aggressively, have an unbearable sore throat after the 10th treatment day or so, lose my ability to taste, likely need a feeding tube, be tired a lot, and not want to speak after week 4 or so. I'm preparing myself for the worst and will face it head on to the best of my ability.

Aug 26

At the end of my meeting with Rita yesterday, she asked if I had any other questions. I said that I did. It's what I call the "elephant in the room" question. Everyone has been very positive and optimistic so far. However, no one has said that I'll be cured or that my chances are good or that I'll beat this. After all, I have cancer. And cancer kills. So, I got the courage to ask Rita what the cure rate is for my type of cancer in patients like me. I'm only 54, don't smoke, am in good shape and otherwise healthy. Rita said she'd have to ask Dr. Zachem and would get back to me.

I spoke with her today and got the answer. She had consulted with Dr. Zachem and told me that he felt like I have a "better than 2/3's chance of being cured." I was hoping for 80% or better, but at least it's not less than 50%. I'm a gambling man and I'll take those odds. I'm going to work hard at this. It will be my new, full-time job to kick cancer's ass!

Friends' Comments:

Tara L.
Jim,
I feel compelled to write. I have seen friends through cancer, the worst being full-blown skin cancer. I understand it is common that people sometimes end up with a different set of friends through this process, and closer relationships with those existing friends that can be open, honest, listen as you need to share and release, laugh in the face of adversity and cry with you when that is needed. Some people will fall away. They are

uncomfortable. They can't relate for whatever reason. Let them be, even though it may hurt or be hard to do. They can give no more.

Those who bring you things you need will come in different forms. Some of them will wear angel's wings. Some of them will provide laughter and an escape. Some of them will send a card to brighten your day. Some will make you a meal and deliver or send your favorite treats. Some will keep you involved in the normal aspects of life (like including you in the latest..like an ice bucket challenge), wanting you to realize life is the same, as different as it is, and you are included! Some will only be able to act normal, rather than reach out more intimately, because of their discomfort, but they remain in your life. Some will simply say hello, and you may not know them at all, but they follow your post and support you. And you will smile that gorgeous Jim Petzing smile. Love and caring will come differently than before. It will be richer when rich, and poorer when poor. Cancer is not allowed to rob your heart and soul. You will be at once blessed, and stunned, but you have no energy to morn those who you thought were friends. Through it all you will know love deeper than ever, know caring and healing more than imagined, and know that anything causing pain, including cancer, receives no homage and can simply leave. :-)

Brian C.

Jim, you will beat this! They always underestimate so that you can over deliver. And you will. I'm sorry you didn't get the one-on-one that you wanted on Sunday. There are friends, and then there are angels. You know the difference.

Kristin A.

You ARE making such a positive impact by sharing your journey, Jim. Every day I am reminded how BLESSED we are in so many ways ... thank you for making my daily journey more joyful. And on a silly note, I'm glad that Beehive transported you away for a few hours. The women are so, so talented -- and a lovely group of humans to boot! Glad we could be a small part of the positive side of the journey.

Paula H.
Jim, You can - and WILL - absolutely do this and beat cancer. Continued prayers for strength and grace during your journey.

Chapter 9

SUCH A FUN DAY WITH MY ZING FAMILY!

MY STAFF AT ZING HAS worked very hard this summer. Scott and I thought it would be fun to have our team outing at Michigan's Adventure (amusement and water park), which is just an hour away. So we closed the restaurant today and 22 of us spent a great day swimming, sunning, eating, laughing and riding crazy fun rides. I don't like heights, so I was really proud of myself for taking on the Wildcat and Corkscrew roller coasters, along with the very high water slide. I'm all about overcoming obstacles right now, so I felt good about conquering those rides as silly as that may sound. It was a super day! Can't wait to do it again next year.

Friends' Comments:

Chris F.
Next year you're riding the Thunder Jack! After your battle with cancer, you can conquer anything!

Karen/Mike Z.
Not silly at all! I'm afraid of heights myself. Conquering a fear is quite rewarding! Keep smiling.

Patty J.
Looking for the LIKE button! I applaud your bravery...my kids would love it if I could do a Tower of Terror or California Adventure with them at Disney. Today you could!

Chapter 10

HOME ALONE...MIND RACING

Aug 30

IT'S SATURDAY MORNING. SCOTT IS opening Zing today, so I slept in until 9am. That's late for me. I've been trying to sleep more, so I'm fully rested when my radiation/chemo treatments start on Tuesday. Honestly, I can't believe that this is all happening. It has been less than two months (53 days to be exact) since I found the lump on the left side of my neck while shaving one morning in Vegas (July 8). Everything has happened so fast. I've done my best to embrace the situation by staying positive and throwing myself into my normal work routine. I'm glad its Labor Day Weekend. We're going to be very busy at Zing the next couple of days and that helps take my mind off things. I still feel great physically, yet my cancer is growing and moving every day in my neck region. I can tell. I'm ready to get going with my treatments, but am anxious. When I'm home alone, like I am now, my mind races. I can't control it. It just does. What will chemo be like? What if they miss my vein? Will I have nausea? How tired I am going to be in the first week? Will I be able to work? Will I feel claustrophobic in my radiation mask? Will I get mouth sores? How long will it be before my throat really starts hurting and I can't swallow easily? Will I need a feeding tube? These are just a few of the many random thoughts that continually flow through my mind. I've always been good at compartmentalizing and putting things in a box when I need to, but I can't seem to harness these thoughts. They're running wild and I want to cage them up. My chemo doc prescribed Ativan for anxiousness. I haven't taken it yet, but am thinking about it. I'm told it also helps with nausea, too. It will probably become a good friend soon.

On a positive note, I'm feeling so good about how folks have been reaching out and asking me how I am doing or if they can do anything to help. My angels, Scott and Elizabeth, are putting a ride schedule together for my daily trips to The Cancer Center and I'm sure they'll be contacting many of my friends to help with the 35 visits I'll be making to Wyoming, MI over the next seven weeks. Elizabeth is taking me on Tuesday for my four hour chemo/radiation treatment. I'm so happy about that. I've also decided to keep my surgery consult/evaluation with Dr. Prince at the University of Michigan next Thursday at 9am. Scott and I will be leaving for Ann Arbor around 6am. My appointment there will last for three hours and then we'll drive to The Cancer Center for my 3pm radiation treatment. It will be a long day and I'm so appreciative that Scott is going with me. The more I can be with others, the better off I will be.

TO BE CONTINUED....

Friends' Comments:

Dale M. & Arthur P.

Oncologists nowadays have a pretty good handle on many of the more unpleasant side effects of chemotherapy, particularly nausea, and the emphasis is on preventing it instead of trying to control it. Before they start the chemotherapeutic agents flowing, they will give you big IV doses of steroids and antiemetics to prevent nausea from developing and to reduce its severity if it develops anyway. Oncology nursing personnel are generally Angels on Earth, skilled not only at finding the portal of a worn out vein but also at finding the portal of your worn out spirits and nurturing it.

In my own cancer treatment experience, I found that once the anticipation of the unknown was over, and the reality of treatment began, it became valuable and important for me to stop trying to control my situation and just let go and have faith that I was being cared for by capable and caring people. Also, chemotherapy is most often administered in communal treatment rooms, with a number of other patients being treated at the same time. I found something very reassuring and bolstering about that, with the understanding that I was not alone, and it was not all about me. There was a Broadway celebrity there, and there was a lady who shoed horses. There was a man who ate his brown bag lunches during his treatments. There was a lady who complained one day that "My hair is falling out....and I don't mean just on my head." Another patient announced one day, "Today's my birthday, and I had nipple rings put in to celebrate." On the other hand I moved along from week to week next to a few people who seemed to be hanging on by thin threads, but I was impressed by the noble dignity of their endurance, which kept me mindful of the saying: "Pain is inevitable, but suffering is optional."

I have a good friend right here in Saugatuck who had the same condition as you and underwent similar treatment plus surgery. And, to be honest, he went through several months of misery during treatment, but today he is as good as new and disease free. I hope you have the same outcome, but without the miserable months. Remember, in any case, that there is life after 2014 and you should enjoy something about every single day from now on... even the lousy days.

Elizabeth B.

Tuesday will come and go and we will make it the best day possible! Try to stay present and take things one step at a time. We will love you through this process and lift you up with positive thoughts and prayers. You are strong in body and mind and we'll kick cancers butt together! Love you, xoxo

Fran M.

All good things are surrounding you and praying for you. Sending energy your way. We love you, Jim, and are by your side even when you can't see us!

Chapter 11

IT ALL STARTS TOMORROW

Sept 1

I'M IN BED NOW TOSSING and turning, so I've decided to make a journal entry. We had a great Labor Day Weekend at Zing. Business was really good and ahead of last year for the same timeframe. It kept my mind focused on other things, but now I'm thinking about tomorrow. I'm really ready to get started with my radiation and chemo treatments. Tuesdays will be my "long" day when I get both chemo and radiation at the same time. The other weekdays will be radiation only. I'm going to have my picture taken each day before treatment starts. I think it will be interesting to see how my body physically changes during the seven weeks. It may not be pretty, but I'm curious to track it. I may decide that this is a bad idea two or three weeks from now, so we'll have to wait and see.

I've still got a bit more reading to do, including pamphlets titled: Radiation Therapy - What It Is and How It Helps, Chemotherapy and You, Living With Cancer A Day at a Time, and Confronting Cancer with a Spirit of Hope. I've had many folks, including my Mom, say to "Take each day one at a time." And, "Don't project, try not to look ahead." I find that so hard to do. I've always been a planner with vision and long term goals. I know that I need to live in the moment now, but it's so hard to not think about the future. And, I really want to be around to enjoy it!

I found out in a text this weekend from my ex-partner Matt, that our cat Magic, is riddled with cancer too and likely doesn't have long to live. I'm sick about it. He's such a loving, good, sweet and amazing cat. We decided that it was best for Magic to stay with Matt when we broke up because he was an older cat set in his ways and we didn't want to disrupt his life. Plus, Magic can't travel in a car without howling at the top of his lungs, hyperventilating, and simultaneously getting very sick at "both ends." It's not pretty. He loved Matt, and Matt grew to love him, so it all worked out. Matt says, that per the veterinarian, Magic is not in any pain. He's managing okay now, but is quickly losing a lot of weight.

Cancer is just a miserable disease. I wonder how much weight I'm going to lose over the next couple of months? For the past two or three weeks, I've been eating all of my favorite foods so as to put on a few pounds in preparation for the inevitable weight loss I'll be experiencing shortly. Eating, drinking, swallowing, talking, kissing and breathing through my mouth are going to become quite difficult in the next few weeks once the treatments take effect. Both sides of my neck, my mouth, and the back of my throat at the base of my tongue where my cancer originated, are going to get blasted with intense doses of radiation. The chemo will accelerate the effects of the radiation. Let the fun begin! Well, I guess I should really try to fall asleep. Long day tomorrow. Elizabeth will be here to pick me up at 10:30am for our drive to The Cancer Center in Wyoming, MI. Sleep well friends.

TO BE CONTINUED......

Friends' Comments:

Scott S.
We are all here for you, Jim. Thanks for your courage!

Josephine B.
You are in our prayers today. We send you loving energy. Even though the road is rocky now, it is still the road to your recovery. Jodi and Chris

Debbie W.

The first step is often the hardest. Today will be your "giant leap" and I know you'll feel a huge sense of relief getting started! We'll be thinking of you. Doug and Debbie

John T.

You've got what it takes! You'll be in our thoughts.

Gerrie B.

May you find some comfort in knowing our thoughts are with you on this journey. Don't try to think you can "man" your way through this. Take the drugs they offer. Take only one day at a time and know we are walking right alongside you. Love you!!

Monica L.

Jim, I just want to give you a big hug and hope the treatment will give you minimal discomfort.

Chapter 12

BACK TO SCHOOL FOR MOST, START OF TREATMENT FOR ME

Sept 2

I WOKE UP THIS MORNING to the news featuring Back to School stories. I couldn't help but smile and reminisce about my first days of school, especially at a new one. Growing up, I attended five different grammar schools from kindergarten through 8th grade. The first day was always filled with nervousness, wonder, excitement, and the hope that I'd like my teachers, make friends fast and fit in. Today was my first day of cancer treatment at The Cancer Center. Fortunately, I already had the orientation, before attending the "required courses", and had a chance to meet the staff that would be administering my chemo and radiation over the next seven weeks.

Elizabeth picked me up this morning and drove me to "campus". They were waiting, greeted me by name, and seated us in the comfy waiting area with a tv, plush leather couches, and pillows. Quickly, my name was called. I weighed in fully clothed at 229 lbs. I've been eating a lot and trying to gain weight knowing I'll lose a lot of pounds in the next month or so. Then I had my blood tested, which is standard each time I have chemo so they can prepare the right chemo formula for me.

The Cancer Center has a group chemo room where there were seven or eight patients "dripping" together, but I wanted a private room so Elizabeth and I could chat and do some Business Association work. They ran a little behind on my scheduled chemo appointment, so the radiation technician came and got me. I laid on the hard, long, flat table and put in the two bite wings, which kept my mouth and tongue stable. The technician unveiled and put on my customized "green hornet" mask that covered my head and neck area. She tightened it on both sides by screwing it into two mini table vices. I extended my arms outward and held onto the wrist grips, like you'd see on a rowing machine. I was told to lie still. This may sound morbid, but it's like you're sitting in an electric chair with a mask covering your face, but you're lying down and locked in and unable to move an inch. The whole apparatus and set up is quite "Star Wars-ish". Surprisingly, I was asked to choose my music from Pandora, but couldn't think of anything but Pharrell. I love his "Happy" song.

Radiation bursts are timed to hit the many different targeted cancer spots during the 25 minute or so treatment. I didn't feel anything except the table moving backward and forward and up and down. I kept my eyes shut and tried to relax, repeating a mantra that soothes me. I'm pretty good with self hypnosis and almost got there. Before I knew it, I was up and out and headed back to my chemo treatment room. I sat in my Lazy Boy recliner and was covered with two warm blankets. Elizabeth brought her computer and two phones (one work and one personal) and we got started talking about business association stuff, while my first med bag of five was hooked into my IV. The chemo technician, Jessica, found a good vein on the top side of my right wrist and hit it right the first time. Good job, Jess!

Bag 1 was saline (15 mins), Bag 2 was anti-nausea meds (20 mins), Bag 3 was a Benedryl/Pepsid combo (20 mins), Bag 4 was Taxol (chemo med #1 for 75 mins) and last, but not least, Bag 5 was Carboplatin (chemo med #2 for 75 mins). The process lasted for 3 1/2 hours or so. Good news is that Bag 3 knocked me out and I slept for about 1hr 45 mins. Elizabeth said I even slept through the loud beeper that went off every 10 mins to alert the technician to come increase the drip speed. The only time I woke up was when she sneezed and said, "Do you want a blanket?" We laughed when she told me about that.

Day 1, CHECK! Easy breezy. Hope they're all like this one, even though I know that's wishful thinking. I had so much energy that we went to Sam's Club to stock up on protein shakes, fruit, juices, peanut butter, whey protein, water and some basics I'll need when my throat gets sore and can't eat or drink easily. $273 later we were on our way home. So glad Elizabeth was with me today. I'm making her dinner tonight (cheeseburgers, sautéed spinach, mac & cheese, and ice cream). We're going to watch America's Got Talent...The Semi-Finals. Love that show! I have radiation tomorrow at 3:10pm and Scott is taking me. Thanks for all of your prayers and good wishes.

TO BE CONTINUED.....

Friends' Comments:

Brian C.

Jim, you are amazing! Thank you for sharing what you're going through with all of us who love you. Any one of us could be in your shoes right now. It's just the luck of the draw. You're handling it with your incredible strength that I have always admired. Cancer is no match against Jim Petzing!!

Dar W.

I love the "TO BE CONTINUED...." concluding your posts. It means you are ready for what comes next, whatever it brings. Lots of love out here for you, big guy!

Lauren F.

GREAT start. Easy breezy indeed. With your great attitude, treatment will go as smoothly as it can. Remember, Annette is on call for you this month before she leaves for Germany in October. I am here for you as well and will start preparing some easy to eat items.

We send you lots of love and hugs & prayers for healing and inner peace. xoxo,

Lauren & Annette

Elizabeth B.

Jim, Day 1 is behind you...complete with Nap 1! To see you so peaceful during treatment is a testament to the love and support coming your way via prayers, positive thoughts, and special friends reaching out. Live Strong!

Donna F.

Jim, thanks for sharing your first day experience. Glad that Day 1 went as "well" as can be expected. I thought of you all day and will continue to pray daily for continued strength, both physical and mental!

Patty J.

Keep the positive, good news coming!

Chapter 13

Touched by Two Cards Today

Sept 3

I WOKE UP AT 5:30AM and couldn't get back to sleep, so I went to Snap Fitness and ran a 5K on the treadmill in 31:32 (not too bad for not working out in three months). It felt good. My doctors have encouraged me to be as active as I can while doing my treatments. Next week my radiation schedule changes to 10:10am every day, so I'll try to get up and go to the gym at least three times a week, but probably not on Tuesday, which is chemo and radiation day. We'll see how long I can stick to that plan.

Scott took me to radiation today. He saw me get strapped in and got to go behind the scenes to see how they do it. He was fascinated by how the technology works. We wondered how they did radiation 20 to 30 years ago without the technological advancements of today? A little bit of dry mouth and a slight tinny taste on the tongue was evident after the treatment. We ate cookies on the drive home and they went down just fine.

I received two beautiful cards today. One was from John & Vince (friends and regulars at Zing). On the cover of the card was my name and a damask violet with the words "Observant, Protective, and Thoughtful". Inside the card it stated: "In 1863 Sarah Carter, an American author, assigned first names to flowers. Each flower had different words assigned to it. The flower emblem on the front of this card is the flower for that name. Every person, like every flower, is uniquely made and loved by God. Flowers are a gift from God, bringing peace and goodwill. They teach us about life and death, patience and gratitude, mystery and beauty."

Along with this sentiment was a note that said, "A Triduum of Masses will be offered for Jim Petzing on September 1, 2 & 3." A triduum is a three-day period of prayer that recalls the three days that Christ spent in the tomb, from Good Friday until Easter Sunday. I was really moved by this.

Another card I received today was from Pastor Sal and the Douglas Congregational UCC (United Church of Christ). Interestingly, I grew up attending a Congregational Church in Naugatuck, CT where I was President of our youth group and rang bells in a handbell choir for eight years. I have such fond memories of those days, but for some reason I never continued on with regular attendance at church as an adult. Pastor Sal wrote a personal note that included the following: "Many of us at Douglas UCC have been patrons of Zing for many years now, so please know that there's a church full of people each Sunday sending healing thoughts of love and light your way". I was very touched and am planning to attend the 10am service this Sunday with my friends Jodi and Chris who invited me to attend with them. I'm excited to go and explore my faith and spirituality again.

On the front of Pastor Sal's card, it said: "Everything that happens in this life is a gift. Even as you struggle through this difficult time, you are gaining strength and wisdom that will help you further down the road. Remember, no matter what happens, you'll always have people that care for you." I really believe that I have many people in this community that care about me. I'm so thankful to be living here during my battle with cancer. I actually think that this was a reason why I was supposed to move here and not be in a big city, like Chicago, anymore. I've always thought that our ultimate destiny is pre-planned, but that life is full of detours that a higher power has laid out for us to experience in different ways. Some of these detours will be joyous, while others will be a struggle, like I'm faced with now. Together they give us an appreciation for the gift of life. Perhaps this is my time to better understand that gift? I hope that I'll be able to leverage that gift in a meaningful way for others when I win this battle with cancer.

TO BE CONTINUED....

Friends' Comments:

Charlene P.

Amen to that. Truer words are so seldom spoken. Each and every day is a gift and one which we should always cherish. Thanks, Jim, for sharing your journey. You are an inspiration to many! Keep that spirit with you always.

Tim H.

Just a fantastic testimonial to your character and spirit. All the best for continued progress and joy in the "gift" you have been given. With you every day in thoughts.

Dan G.

Amen!, Jim. Read this and thought of you. Life is strange and wonderful.

"The Poignancy of this Fleeting Moment"

Awareness itself is the primary currency of the human condition and, as such, deserves to be spent carefully. Sitting quietly in a serene environment, letting go of the various petty disturbances that roil and diminish consciousness, and experiencing as fully as possible the poignancy of this fleeting moment—this is an enterprise of deep intrinsic value, an aesthetic experience beyond words.

- Andrew Olendzki, "Busy Signal"

Donna F.

Jim, even going through life challenges, God continues to give us the support we need! And, it is obvious that you are supported by many blessings of good friends and prayers. Thanks for your update and you are giving me an incentive to WORK OUT!

Lauren F.

Great post, Jim! Every day is a gift. Sometimes it takes a while to realize it.

Chapter 14

On the Right Track

Sept 4

SCOTT PICKED ME UP AT 6am. We drove 2 hours and 45 minutes in the pouring rain to Ann Arbor for my consult with Dr. Mark Prince at the University of Michigan Hospital. I'm really glad I kept this appointment. Dr. Prince specializes in neck cancer surgery. If my chemo/radiation treatments don't do the job, he would be the surgeon to operate on me. The good news is that Dr. Prince fully believes that I'm on the right track. He also would have recommended doing the chemo/radiation combo treatment first, before getting involved with surgery.

Based on his review of my case and his experience with other patients like me, he thinks there's a good chance (67-80%) that the aggressive chemo/radiation I'm receiving over the next seven weeks will eradicate the cancer. If for some reason the treatments fail to remove it, the tumors should be much smaller and, in turn, easier to remove via surgery. Dr. Prince and his team spent about 75 minutes with me. We reviewed all the possible scenarios and the resulting steps that would need to be taken for each. I feel more informed and confident that I've made the right decisions so far.

Our drive back to Douglas was a lot easier as the bad weather had cleared. Scott dropped me off at home and I caught up on emails for a half hour. Then, I drove myself to Wyoming and The Cancer Center for my radiation treatment. I felt fine and didn't need anyone to go with me. For some reason, I felt a bit claustrophobic on the table today and my heart was beating faster than usual. I got through the 25 minute treatment and then met with Dr. Bott, who was filling in for Dr. Julie. Thursday is "Doctor Day" when you meet with your radiation oncologist after your radiation treatment. Dr. Julie was off today, so Dr. Bott filled in. She was very nice and had the tough discussion with me about how I'm going to feel at the end of Week 3 after 14 radiation and 3 chemo treatments. Given that I'm being blasted by radiation on both sides of my neck, in my mouth and at the base of my tongue, Dr. Bott thinks I'm going to have an extremely difficult time swallowing, drinking and eating.

She suggested that I have a consult in the next week or so with the doctor that would do the operation to insert a feeding tube, if I need one. Dr. Bott recommended that I seriously consider getting the feeding tube inserted before the end of Week 3. By doing the procedure sooner than later, it likely can be put in down through my esophagus and out through my stomach versus being surgically inserted into my stomach by cutting through the outside of it. The first option is only possible if my throat isn't too swollen to get the tube down. After Week 3, I'm told that becomes much more difficult and the latter option is the standard approach. Additionally, Dr. Bott said that getting the feeding tube inserted while I'm not feeling so sick will be much easier than when I'm barely able to eat, drink, or swallow and feel like I have a horrible flu along with the worst sore throat ever.

After Dr. Bott, I met with Deb, the dietician, and we had a similar conversation. She also reinforced how important it will be for me to be consistently hydrated and nourished during my treatments, so that proper healing can take place. Deb also thought the feeding tube was a good idea, so I asked her to get my consult set up. I then drove home, took an hour nap, and went to work. We had a rehearsal dinner for 32 people tonight on our garden patio at Zing. It went very smoothly. We were also nicely busy with a number of other tables in the dining room. lounge and lounge patio, so it was a great night. I'm falling asleep while writing this entry, so off to bed I go.

Friends' Comments:

Dar W.

Jimbo, seems like the decision to get the feeding tube in sooner than later is a good one. Straight talk from a doctor makes one vulnerable, but it is invaluable. Healing prayers big guy!

Chapter 15

Just a Little Tired....and Queasy

Sept 5

FINISHED DAY 4 OF RADIATION today. I only have six more chemo and 31 more radiation treatments to go! ARGH. I have a calendar that I mark off with a Big "X" at the end of each treatment day. It's a bit daunting to think I'm just over 10% done. Elizabeth went with me this afternoon and took pictures of "Henry". I'm not sure why I named the radiation machine "Henry"? I guess I felt it needed a name since I'm going to be spending a lot of time with it. LOL. I think you'd be surprised if you could see what "Henry" looks like. He's quite large and techno-advanced. Elizabeth has taken pictures of me being consumed by "Henry". They remind me of the old Frankenstein movies. I'm lying prone on a hard table, covered with a white blanket (because it's so damn cold in the radiation room), holding onto wrist straps that keep my shoulders down and body tight, and wearing a "glow in the dark" green mesh mask that covers my entire head down to my shoulders. It's quite a sight to behold.

I was told yesterday that the chemo I had on Tuesday may start to affect me two to three days later. Well, it certainly did. I had to take two, one hour naps today before and after radiation. My body just needed to sleep. I was also informed that different smells and tastes may set off a feeling of nausea. Well, that happened too. While working at Zing tonight, the smell of our BBQ Baby Back Ribs (my favorite year-round item on the menu) made me want to hurl. When I was chatting with a table of six guests, where five of them were enjoying the ribs, I had to excuse myself.

A wave of nausea came over me, but I didn't throw up. I should have taken my anti-nausea pill before going to work. I'll be doing that for now on. The week definitely caught up with me, so I ended up going home at 10pm.

Friends' Comments:

Gerrie B.

Great idea to name the linear accelerator Henry. Now, when you are lying on the table, use visual imagery on how Henry is zapping all the cancer cells but leaving all the healthy cells and tissues. Each day brings you closer to feeling like your old self. I have seen so many success stories with the same type of cancer.

Chapter 16

FELT REALLY GOOD TODAY

Sept 6

My sleeping pill (Zolpidem) works great! I got about eight hours last night and woke up at 7am. I had to open Zing this morning as we're still serving breakfast and lunch, along with dinner, on Friday through Monday. We still have dinner on Thursday nights, too, but are closed on Tuesday and Wednesday now. It's nice not being open seven days a week, like we were this summer for 2 1/2 months. I got to Zing at 8am, did the closing of the books for last night, and started setting up the lounge patio for outdoor diners. Our server/bartender usually arrives at 8:45am, but not today. At 9:30am, I was still solo. I was worried about having to manage alone, especially if we got busy, so I called Scott and he came in to help. I'm glad I did as we had a steady flow of guests and we both made about $70 in tips working as servers. Drinking money for the future. LOL.

I had a lot of energy this morning. Scott and I were a good team. We came to find out later that our server/bartender had an unfortunate altercation with the law last evening, was detained overnight, and not able to call us. All is fine now. We worked until 4pm and then our evening staff arrived. I went home and took an hour nap. Before heading back to work, I stopped by "Live Art, Live Music" on Center Street in Douglas. A nice crowd was forming. I wrote and taped the :60 radio spot for the event and was so pleased to see the excitement and renewed energy for the downtown area. The weather couldn't have been better. We had a calm, but decent, night at Zing. I had taken my anti-nausea pill, so all went well. I got home at 11:45pm and passed out on my couch while watching Saturday Night Live. Overall, I felt really good today!

Friends' Comments:

Lauren F.

Wow, quite a day. You're a strong man!

Star & Charlie

You are soooo awesome and caring! Our continued prayers. Love love LOVE you!

Karen/Mike Z.

One week down...A few or so more to go. You can do it. Our continued thoughts and prayers.

Chapter 17

SUPPORTED BY FRIENDS NEAR & FAR, OLD & NEW

Sept 7 & 8

THESE TWO DAYS HAVE BEEN filled with joyous, heartwarming, and touching experiences with both new and old friends. On Sunday, I was invited to attend church at the Douglas United Church of Christ with Jodi and Chris, a wonderful couple that frequents my restaurant. I've been thinking about getting back into regular church going, so this was the perfect opportunity to do so. Jodi and Chris picked me up at 9:45am and we attended the 10am service. I immediately felt comfortable as I knew many folks in the congregation of 100 or so, as well as Pastor Sal. There was beautiful music, singing, prayers and scripture readings, along with a thought-provoking homily by an energizing Pastor Sal. I was stimulated spiritually. After the service, there was coffee, cake, and ice cream outside the church. Everyone was so nice and welcoming. Many knew of my battle with cancer and showed caring and concern. I'll definitely be going back!

After church, I boarded Bernie and Rick's 65ft yacht, the Indigo. I had never been on a private boat like this before. It was absolutely stunning, but even better was the company. There were ten of us in total and we had stimulating conversation during the entire four hour cruise to Lake Maca-tawa in Holland, MI and back. We anchored awhile out in Lake Michigan and took in the absolutely gorgeous day. We waved as other boats passed by. It was just what the doctor ordered for me. I felt invigorated, happy, and relaxed. It took my mind of the Big C for a short time. When I got home, I watched some NFL football games, checked Facebook, and made myself dinner. It was a great day!

This morning I went to the Post Office and a big box was waiting for me. It was from my good high school friend, Ann. We reconnected on Facebook in late Spring/early Summer, along with some other graduates from the Class of '78 at Naugatuck High School (Naugatuck, CT). Ann has been sending me messages on a frequent basis, since learning of my illness. They've been so insightful and inspirational. I've been really moved by Ann's support, especially since I haven't seen or spoken with her in over 30 years. In the box was a care package including: a blanket, sippy cup, suckers, colored pencils, drawing pad, journal, crossword puzzle book, Blistex, hand sanitizers and a $15 Apple iTunes card. What a thoughtful and generous gesture! I also received some very nice cards from other friends today. With an awesome start to the day, I drove myself to radiation and finished Day 5 of 35 treatments.

Friends' Comments:

Duane M.

So happy you had a good weekend. Really glad you enjoyed church and the boost it provides. You are in our thoughts and prayers. Hugs, D&J

William A.

Twas indeed a wonderful day. May every day outshine the other.

Dan G.

Jim, I love reading and seeing how much gratitude you have. I love you and pray for you every day my friend.

Charlene P.

It's so wonderful that so many friends old and new are reaching out to you. What a great feeling knowing so many care and are there to support and pray for you during your treatments. Hold onto those feelings as they will help you get through this. Xoxo

Chapter 18

Moving Right Along

Sept 9

TODAY COULDN'T HAVE GONE BETTER for a five hour chemo/radiation appointment. Elizabeth took me this morning and we got a lot of Business Association work done. I didn't get knocked out by the Pepsid/Benadryl bag like last time because I've been getting a lot of sleep each night (about 8 hours) plus a one hour nap during the day. Negative chemo reactions usually happen two or three days after the treatment, so I have anti-nausea pills I take each morning. It's still a bit weird that I don't feel sick at all, just a little fatigued every now and then.

I met with my social worker, dietician and patient navigator today. All indicated that I will start to feel sick around the end of next week, kind of a "hitting the wall" feeling that comes on fast. I'm hoping I'll be one of those star patients that gets all the way to Week 6 feeling just fine. That would be amazing! My social worker, Tracy, says that those folks also heal faster after treatments end. Please let that be me! She also gave me some interesting insight on the feeding tube. It appears that insurance companies have stopped covering the feeding tube, IF it's inserted as a precaution when feeling well versus a necessity when eating and hydration have stopped. So she recommended that I keep my consult on Thursday, which is a requirement for getting the tube. Then she suggested that I schedule my surgery for ten days from Thursday, which would put me at a time when I likely will not want to (or can't) eat or drink. So insurance would kick in. If I'm doing well and eating/drinking appropriately, then I can move the surgery later if and when I need it. I like this strategy and will likely implement it.

The other interesting thing I learned today is that anyone having chemo must have protected sex. The chemo is a poison that can make others sick, if they are exposed to certain amounts of it. It's even necessary to wipe up urine that hits the toilet seat, so no one sits on it. Wow, who knew? I'm feeling very informed these days.

It looks like the radiation and chemo technicians at The Cancer Center may be planning a going away party for one of their own at Zing on a "Tinis & Teasers" Thursday in the next couple of weeks. That would be fun! I suggested a Monday or Thursday evening. We have HALF-PRICE appetizers and $9 Zingtinis (mega-martinis regularly priced at $12) on Thursday nights. Plus, we make our famous meatloaf only on MEAT-LOAF MONDAYS! For ONLY $19, you get two big pieces, mashed potatoes, veggies, bread, and FREE DESSERT. Our meatloaf was the #1 seller last Fall, Winter and Spring. You will love it, too! I can't help being a marketer even in my posts. LOL.

When I got back to the office to do some work after chemo, the most gorgeous flowers I've ever seen were waiting for me from Julie & Jacqueline. They're on my desk at work now and will be transferred home on Thursday night as I'm taking most of the weekend off to spend with my angel, Chris. I'm very excited to see him. Day 6 of 35 is in the books. Feeling good!

Friends' Comments:

Charlene P.
Thanks so much for your posts. They are so informative and helpful in allowing all of us, who care so much about you, to better understand what you're going through every day. You have always been a great story teller and I admire that quality in you! Keep strong and positive.

Tammy W.

Make up your mind. YOU will be one of those star patients making it to Week 6 feeling just fine. Not a question. Take your glutamine, drink your veggies and cop that positive attitude! No doubts. Understand "I will be one of those people....and may even raise the bar." You are fighting a big fight. The Big C doesn't win! And, Hope is watching by the sidelines. The "I will fuck you cancer, You met the wrong guy, God has his hand on me attitude.. WINS!" I mean that with all the love in the world, from one cancer survivor to another.

John H.

You are a laugh riot, promoting Zing on Caring Bridge. That may be a first! I guess you're not feeling that bad, if you can be writing about Meatloaf! My poor Dad had his chemo when anti-nausea drugs weren't even around. Imagine how horrifying it was for Peggy and the kids to hear my Dad hurling bile every hour while trying to comfort my poor Mother. That was a long time ago, luckily for you. Stay strong, Mr. Zing!

Cory R.

Wow, lots of great info that most of us don't know! Thank you for sharing your journey. It makes the whole damn situation visible, real and doable, instead of a horrific unknown mystery that causes such fear and panic. We love you, Jim, and are thinking you will be one of the star pupils who just sail through with minimal pain and side effects! Xoxo

Chapter 19

Feeding Tube or No Feeding Tube? ...We'll See

Sept 11

Scott drove me to the other side of Grand Rapids today to meet with Dr. William Rozell, at Advanced Radiology Services, for my feeding tube consultation. In preparation for the appointment, I read the pamphlet "Tube Feeding at Home". For the most part, everything we discussed in our short 15 minute appointment was in the pamphlet. Dr. Rozell's opinion was that I likely will need a feeding tube given that I'm being blasted by radiation on both sides of my neck, in my mouth at the back of my throat, and at the base of the tongue. Today is Day 8 of radiation and is the first day I've felt any soreness in my throat since the start of treatments. It feels a little scratchy, but nothing major. I decided to move forward and have his office schedule the operation for insertion of a G-tube in my stomach, but can move or cancel it without a penalty. Basically, it's on the calendar as an insurance policy if I find that I'm unable to drink, eat, and swallow or am losing a lot of weight and getting dehydrated. At this point, that's not a problem as I've purposely been gaining weight and eating anything I want.

I received a call this afternoon indicating that the overnight surgical procedure has been scheduled for next Thursday, September 18 at Metro Health Hospital, one week from today. I have a feeling I'll be moving it to one week later, but we'll see.

After meeting with Dr. Rozell, we headed over to The Cancer Center for my daily radiation. I've been taking a teaspoon full of glutamine (with water), an amino acid, before and after each radiation treatment. My cancer survivor friend, Tammy, said that it helped save her salivary glands during her treatments, so I'm giving it a try. So far, so good! I really like the radiation technicians, especially Courtney and Ashley. I see them every weekday for my 20 minute blast with "Henry", the linear accelerator radiation machine. They get me set up on the table, throw warm blankets on me, give me my bite wings, bolt me into the "green hornet" mask, and have me grab the wrist straps. Away we go.

Thursday is "Doctor Day" so Scott and I met with Rhonda, the radiation nurse, and Dr. Julie Forstner, my radiation oncologist and 4th angel. It was great to see Dr. Julie again as last week I met with another one her colleagues, Dr. Bott, during "Doctor Day". Dr. Julie said I'm progressing along nicely. She felt both sides of my neck and it appears that the right side tumor has shrunk slightly and the larger left side one by a half centimeter. This is a good sign. We talked about the possibility of getting the feeding tube and Dr. Julie thinks it's a 50/50 shot of whether I'll need it or not. She agrees that I should have the operation scheduled on the calendar as an insurance policy, especially since we don't know how sore my throat will be over the next few weeks and how that will affect my eating and drinking. So that's the plan. On a very encouraging note, Dr. Julie mentioned that another one of her patients is on treatment 28 of 35 and is still eating tacos! Please let that be me.

TO BE CONTINUED....

Parkinson’s

Friends' Comments:

Dan C.

Thanks for the updates, Jim! Your outlook and insight into the process is somehow oddly comforting to me because I worry about friends who are dealing with challenges when I don't know what's up. Thanks for comforting me! LOL I know it likely wasn't your goal, but it's working. Big ole hugs to you!

Chapter 20

Glad Chris is Here!

Sept 12

I HAVEN'T BEEN ABLE TO spend quality time with Chris for two weeks, so I'm really happy that he's here hanging with me through the weekend. Chris went with me to radiation today and got to meet my new girlfriends (the radiation technicians) and see "Henry", the linear accelerator, in action. Afterwards, we saw the suspense thriller, "No Good Deed". It was just okay. We headed home and napped for two hours. I was exhausted. By Friday, I'm kind of spent after a week of radiation and chemo treatments, and trying to maintain a normal work schedule. Last Friday was my worst day so far, as the Tuesday chemo took effect and caused me to feel a bit nauseous. It happened again today. I got nauseous after our nap, so I took one of my pills and am hoping to feel better. I'm glad I'm not working at Zing tonight because I really have no energy. It will be nice to sleep in tomorrow morning, too. Chris is making himself some chili for dinner and so far the smell isn't bothering me. I'm hoping I'll get my appetite back this evening. I always feel good when Chris is around.

TO BE CONTINUED....

Friends' Comments:

Dar W.
Ain't it grand to have a loving supportive partner?

Thomas F.

Jim, just had a chance to sign onto Caring Bridge. The number of visits on your blog say it all. Wow, in a short space of time you already have 1064 visits. That is 1064 times someone has had the time just to sign onto the site, let alone the HUGE multiple that number represents in how many times someone has shared a thought or said a prayer. You have a lot of support on this walk. What a testimony to you, your circle of friends and family, and the strength of the circle that is there for you!

Chapter 21

Running Out of Steam

Sept 13 & 14

I HAD A GREAT WEEKEND with Chris. It was so good to spend quality time with him. We don't get to see a lot of each other, so we always try to maximize our time together. Plus, we both know that I'm not going to be feeling well very soon. I took Friday and Saturday off from work. This was a good thing as I hit the wall on Friday and was incredibly lethargic on Saturday. Sleep is a necessity for me now. I used to be able to get by on an average of 6 hours, but not anymore. Friday night I slept 9 1/2 hours and complemented it with a 2 1/2 hour nap on Saturday. Then, Saturday night I got 8 1/2 hours of sleep.

Mornings are when I have the most energy, so I was able to go to the gym with Chris on Saturday morning and work our Sunday Brunch at Zing. We had 130 guys join us from the Lambda Car Club (our third time hosting them), plus our regular Sunday morning guests. Scott did an amazing job coordinating the two buffets and getting everything set up. All went smoothly and I'm glad I was there to help out.

Chris got me set up on Netflix this weekend, so I'm looking forward to being able to watch more of the shows I want when I'm home on the couch. I'm also trying to get caught up on the series, Revenge, so we can watch Season 3 together. I just love Madelaine Stowe's character, Victoria Grayson, and the overall premise of this show.

Chris made us an Asian Chicken Salad for dinner last night and I made him watch the Miss America Pageant with me. No judging here, please. I've loved all of the pageants since I was a kid. Miss New York took the crown for the third year in a row and stunned the crowd with a very casual, sitting on the floor, "slap the cup" routine singing to Pharrell's "Happy" song. I preferred the ventriloquist performance of Miss Ohio singing "Supercalafragilisticexpialadocious" with her muppet-type puppet, but that didn't get her in the top 5. Our favorite was Miss Mississippi, a former American Idol Top 1 3, but she only got into the top 1 0.

It was a super weekend, but I'm starting to not feel like myself. I'm constantly tired and just don't have a whole lot of energy. Plus, my throat is really starting to hurt. I expected this, but was hoping I'd have a little more time before feeling this way. I'm going to try to maintain my normal schedule this coming week, but I feel like I'm running out of steam. ARGH.

TO BE CONTINUED....

Friends' Comments:

Charlene P.
Allow your body to tell you what you need. Resting and sleep are really good now as they will guide you through this. Hugs and prayers are sent your way. XO!

Dar W.
Sleeping is good. Hope you are getting your feeding tube in sooner than later.

Tammy W.
Thinking of you! Rest is good for healing. Drink as many greens as you can. It's your time to catch up on movies, favorite shows, read and rest when you need it. Take care!

Gerrie B.

Your body needs all the rest it can get to start the healing process, so know that while you're resting you are busy rebuilding healthy cells and gobbling up the destructive ones. Think of it like a PacMan game. Missed seeing you Saturday night at Zing, but happy to know Scott is taking such good care of you. Know that my thoughts and love are with you as you continue on your journey.

John T.

Sounds like you are being realistic and in-tune with your body's reaction to the treatment. Good coaches and good student. Perfect combination.

Chapter 22

THROAT ON FIRE

Sept 15

WOW, I CAN'T REMEMBER THE last time I had a sore throat like this. My docs and nurses were right. They said that during Week 3, between treatments #12 to 15, it generally gets really tough for bilateral neck and base of tongue radiation/chemo patients. Today was #10 of 35 radiation treatments for me, and it feels like my throat was lit on fire. I'm trying not to freak out too much, but the thought of having a sore throat like this (or worse) for five more weeks of treatment, and a couple of months afterwards, isn't sitting well with me. I didn't sleep at all last night because I also have a nasty post nasal drip that, when lying flat in bed, makes it difficult to get comfortable. So, I took a sleeping pill, propped myself up with pillows, and gave it my best shot. I worked a full day today before going to radiation, which was delayed until 4:10pm because "Henry" was having technical problems again. While at radiation, I met with the nurses to get advice on how best to handle my sore throat. I was told to start taking my pain medication, Norco. When I did, it definitely relieved some of the rawness and made it a little easier to eat a PBJ sandwich for dinner. I was also given a numbing liquid which I'm supposed to mix with water and sip through a straw, so it hits the back of my throat and doesn't numb my mouth. I'll try that tonight before I go to bed and take it with both a pain pill and sleeping pill. Hopefully, I'll get a good night's sleep. Elizabeth is picking me up tomorrow morning at 9am for chemo/radiation day. Not looking forward to the five hours at The Cancer Center, but it will be nice to spend some quality time with Elizabeth.

TO BE CONTINUED....

Friends' Comments:

Jeanne S.

Did they give you the "magic mouthwash?" My sister was given that and it helped quite a bit. That is literally what it is called. Praying for your recovery. Just please keep a positive attitude that you will win, even though at times you don't feel that you can.

Dan G.

Jim, I hate reading about your suffering. Try to stay in "the now" and not think beyond it. Hang in there you good soul.

Chapter 23

DECIDED ON THE TUBE

Sept 16

I DIDN'T SLEEP VERY WELL last night. The constant phlegm production and drip down the back of my already sore throat drove me crazy. I took two Benedryl, along with my pain pill, to try to dry things up and reduce the soreness. That only worked temporarily. I was finally able to fall asleep propped up with three pillows behind my head. My saliva has now become viscous-like and accumulates in my mouth because it's so hard to swallow. I find myself constantly spitting into Kleenex or paper towels, especially when my pain pill wears off.

When I got up this morning, I knew I had to eat but my throat was too sore for anything substantive. I decided to have a small cup of cold vanilla pudding, which actually tasted good and felt really soothing on my throat. I think it will become a staple in my new diet, along with milk shakes, scrambled eggs with cheese, mashed potatoes, chicken soup with tiny chicken pieces, broccoli cheddar soup, and mac & cheese. I also have discovered Muscle Milk and Boost and am enjoying them as much as one can. They're loaded with protein and are nutrient rich. Elizabeth picked me up at 9am for our 40 minute drive to Wyoming, my second home. She had a strawberry banana smoothie and a cup of coffee waiting for me in the car. Elizabeth is so thoughtful and caring. The smoothie had a straw so I went for it, but it just didn't sit well with me. I've developed some mouth sores on the inside of my lips that really sting when fruits or anything acidic passes over them. Also, "citrus" doesn't taste good to me anymore. I was told by my docs and nurses that some smells and tastes I used to like will not be pleasing to my palate any longer, and vice versa.

Radiation is getting tougher to handle now because I'm lying completely flat on my back with a sore throat and a constant phlegm drip that makes me want to gag. I'm also in a claustrophobic mask with bite wings in my mouth. It's so hard not to cough or move, let alone breathe. The Ativan does a good job at relaxing me, so that's now a constant before radiation. After today's treatment, I had my blood pressure taken. It was way higher than normal, about 137 over 92. The change in how I feel I'm sure is playing a prominent role.

Dr. Zachem, my chemo oncologist, came in and spoke with us. He prescribed the same pain medication for me again, but this time in a liquid form. This will be so much easier than swallowing that big pill, which I've been splitting in half lately. Dr. Z also encouraged me to go for the feeding tube. He said that eating, drinking and swallowing is likely going to get much worse for me, especially if I'm already rating my pain a 7 out of 10 without the pain pill. I was hoping that I could avoid the feeding tube for a while longer, but I can't imagine being able to consume the 2000 to 2500 calories the dietician told me I'm supposed to have each day. For example, I've only had 400 calories so far today and am not sure what I want for dinner. Plus, Fridays and Saturdays are really bad days for me when the steroids from the chemo wear off and I have very little energy or appetite.

I discussed the situation with my chemo nurse, Jessica, and she also agreed that I probably would do better with the feeding tube given my current "not so good" situation and her experience working with patients like me. So, after my hour-long chemo nap and praying for the right answer, I decided to go forward with the feeding tube surgery this Thursday at Metro Health Hospital. The surgery is scheduled for 1pm and my check in is at noon. The procedure will take one hour. I will be kept overnight for observation and to learn how to properly use the feeding tube to supplement whatever eating I'm able to do on my own. During chemo today, I covered myself with a beautiful "prayer blanket" that was crocheted by one our regular Zing guests, Marilyn. She and her husband, Mike, are so sweet. I'm really touched by their gift and plan to take the blanket with me to the hospital on Thursday!

Friends' Comments:

Doug G.
Thinking of you daily and sending positive healing thoughts.

Charlene P.
Hang in there, Jim. The road ahead will be lumpy. But knowing that you are loved and prayers for strength are coming your way from so many will get you through this. The feeding tube will keep your body nourished. I will be praying that your Thursday surgery goes well. Xoxo

Tammy W.
Jim, I'm so sorry to hear of your struggles with the reaction to radiation and chemo. You will need to keep up your strength using any means necessary and it sounds like the feeding tube is going to be a vehicle to help you do that. I remember the mask and the mouth guards..and how difficult it got to lie still. Xanax became my friend. You're in my prayers!

Janie F.
Oh Jim, so very sorry that you are having to go through this struggle. So admire your strength.

Chapter 24

FEELING SPIRITUAL

Sept 17

WEDNESDAY HAS BECOME MY BEST day of the week. The steroids from chemo relieve some of the soreness in my throat and give me some much needed energy. Even though I only have minor relief for a day, I'll take it. I had a productive day at work, did some laundry, and got a lot of errands accomplished after having my morning radiation treatment. It felt good to feel good.

The highlight of my day was my meeting with Pastor Sal from the Douglas UCC. I attended Sunday services there for the first time a week and a half ago with my friends Jodi and Chris, who recommended I give it a try. I really enjoyed myself and was excited to meet with Pastor Sal to get to know him better. The Douglas UCC is only a five minute walk from my home. It was built in the early 1800s and oozes charm, grace and peacefulness. Pastor Sal and I met across the street in the church's Retreat House, where his office is located. Sal greeted me with a big smile and hug. I was curious to understand his religious background, how he became an interfaith minister, and his vision for the Douglas UCC. Plus, I just wanted to get to know him personally as we've seen each other around town and at my restaurant over the years, but have never really had an indepth conversation. I immediately felt comfortable with Pastor Sal and we chatted for over an hour. I felt spiritually invigorated and plan to become a regular church goer.

I've really missed not having church in my life since I was in high school. Although I'm not especially religious, I do consider myself to be quite spiritual and believe in the concept of a higher power or "light" that is guiding us. So, I've been trying to come to grips with why the Big C was placed in MY life's path. Is it a curse? Is it a gift? Is it both? Why me? I want to believe that we're only confronted with life challenges or extremely difficult situations that our higher power is confident we can handle or battle. Perhaps this fullness of experiences, good and bad, will help us become better, more empathetic, and/or more knowing persons? Perhaps, then, it will enable me to make more meaningful differences in the lives of others? I'm stimulated by the possibilities.

TO BE CONTINUED....

Friends' Comments:

BJM

I think you are right. Your situation actually helps you, and everyone else around you, learn lessons and spiritually evolve. I agree that it's not just about you. We all need to ponder what we can learn.

Charlene P.

From the beginning of your journal posts, I have felt that you are not only helping yourself through this process, but also providing valuable information to all of us so we better understand what you're going through every day with your treatments. Cancer is a horrific disease and your posts provide insights that take away some of the fears that all of us have about this frightening disease. Stay strong and positive, Jim. Know that God and many angels are here to help you through this.

Duane M.

So glad you have found a church. Another "Higher" Angel is a good one to have on your team! Our prayers continue for a full recovery.

Thomas F.

Hi Jim, Thanks for your posts. I know they provide us, and I'm sure others, with inspiration. At a time where fear and pain could define your days and message, you have shown clarity and courage. Donna and I think of you everyday and you are held up in prayer.

Chapter 25

The Tube is In

Sept 18

AFTER MUCH DISCUSSION AND DELIBERATION, I decided to have the feeding tube placement surgery. I couldn't fathom the idea of having to choke down 2000 to 2500 calories a day for the next four weeks of chemo/radiation treatment AND the four weeks post-treatment. On the days my throat really hurts, it's bad! It's even difficult to swallow water and get my pills down. Plus, the chemo treatments have left me with virtually no appetite and the radiation has temporarily destroyed most of my taste buds. Nothing tastes right or good. It was inevitable that I would need the feeding tube and I'm glad I got it. Scott spent most of the day with me yesterday. He picked me up at 9:30am and drove me to radiation first and then to the hospital, which is right across from The Cancer Center. Scott is an amazing friend. He hung with me in the pre-op room for about an hour and then waited another 90 minutes until I woke up from my surgery to make sure I was okay. He came up to my overnight room and made sure I was settled before heading out around 3:30pm.

The staff at Metro Health Hospital has been top notch. Everyone I've interacted with has been very helpful and caring. I'm so impressed. I wasn't too anxious about the surgery, as the description I had been given of it by Dr Rozell, the surgeon, and others seemed quite straightforward. Basically, a medium length, narrow plastic tube was inserted at the top of my stomach under my left pectoral about four inches up from by belly button. It hangs down my abdomen about eight inches and has a small opening to insert a gravity drip syringe. The procedure went well, without a hitch. I wasn't allowed to drink or eat anything from midnight the night before until 7:30pm this evening, a total of 19 1/2 hours. My mouth was extremely dry, so I was given a stirrer with a tiny sponge on it that was soaked in water for me to suck on. The docs didn't want anything going in or coming out of my stomach until at least six hours after my surgery, so the healing could begin. I ordered scrambled eggs with cheese, mashed potatoes, and vanilla pudding for dinner and was actually excited to get some food in my system...until it came. The eggs were cold and rubbery and the potatoes tasted like salt, so I ate half of the small cup of vanilla pudding.

My nurse, Laura, came in around 10pm, and taught me how to do my tube feeding. It's pretty easy. First, we stuck the big syringe into the designated hole at the end of the feeding tube, holding it upright, and then added 75ml of water to flush the tube. Then we poured in 120ml of the pre-mixed, nutrient enriched liquid and let it drip through the tube. It took about 12 minutes. When the feeding was completed, we flushed the tube with water again. I couldn't actually feel my stomach filling up with fluid, but I definitely started to feel "full". I think this is going to be a great option for me to keep hydrated and nourished during my treatments and recovery. It's really easy to do. Along with Scott being with me yesterday, my other two angels, Elizabeth and Chris, both came by to visit me post-surgery. Elizabeth brought me a a flowering plant, a stuffed black cat (we named Magic) to keep me company, and a People Magazine. She is so full of good energy and makes me laugh. Chris brought himself and his warm, caring, healing love.

TO BE CONTINUED....

Friends' Comments:

Fred & Janet S.
We are so impressed by your attitude and bravery. Keep it up!

Paula H.
Jim, please know that SO many of us are traveling with you on this journey (thanks to your excellent posts that keep us updated!) and keeping you in our daily prayers.

Cheryl C.
So glad this part of your treatment is in place and already helping you stay strong and nourished.

Sharon L.
I am so glad to hear you are staying positive. I don't know if I could do it. I enjoy and look forward to reading your "story" with each and every post. As you know, or may not remember, we used to go to Sunday school together. I remember you being in the handbell choir. I never understood the white gloves though. And like you, I never went to church after high school.

Several things that have happened during life in general have made me question the existence of a higher power. Now as an adult, I see things differently. Being more spiritual than religious myself, I can understand what you mean. There are worse things people "believe in". It all comes down to one word, FAITH. I had a hard time with that one. Your strength and faith actually help me, believe it or not. Your ability to tell it all and share it with everyone makes me realize that my day to day struggles, which pale in comparison to yours, are not that difficult.

I now treasure each day I wake up and realize what I have. Please don't mistake what I'm saying as feeling sorry for you. I do, but not in a pity type of way. I would not wish what you are going through on anyone. Now I'm not making sense. What I'm trying to say is, you are right. God does give you only what you can handle. And you are handling it great!! Your strength encourages me to not sweat the small stuff. Save my energy for when something big comes along, and have the Faith to trust in a higher power to guide me when the time comes. Kinda like the Footprints in the Sand. Oh, and to always keep a sense of humor. I believe that is important too! Like when I think of those white handbell gloves. God has a sense of humor, too! Stay strong, keep smiling. You are doing great. Ok, I'm done rambling.

Mary Kay B.

You continue to bless each of us by writing your blog. I believe that God (the light, higher power) never promises we won't go through hardships, but he promises to be with us as we go through them. He sends his peace and angels to share our journey. Every time I read your journal, I see proof of this! Your "joy" transcends your situation and I know you are helping so many of us all along the way learn the facts about cancer treatment and how to face a life-threatening diagnosis. Thank you!

Tylor D.

Awesome to hear that despite how much this all sucks, your spirits are up and confidence is certainly clear. It sure seemed like a great idea to go ahead with the feeding tube and I'm glad you moved forward with it. It's also wild to know the process and that you actually can feel full! Keep it up and we are thinking of you.

Chapter 26

40% Done with Treatments, Wish it was Over

Sept 19

I WAS DISCHARGED FROM THE hospital at 12:30pm. My care at Metro Health Hospital, post-surgery and during the night, was excellent. I had a nice room and was very comfortable there, although I didn't sleep much from the tenderness in my stomach caused by the insertion of the feeding tube. Scott picked me up and took me over to The Cancer Center for my 14th of 35 radiation treatments. I'm officially 40% done now. That's the good news! The bad news is that my taste buds are shot, I have no appetite, my throat is a festival of pain, I'm constantly tired, and I can barely eat, drink or swallow. I'm really glad I got the feeding tube. It will make a huge difference in my healing.

Ann, the home care nurse from the "feeding" company, came over to my place at 4:30pm for additional feeding tube training. She brought a month's supply (96 cans) of Jevity (a high protein packed, nourishment liquid that looks a bit like condensed milk) and a bunch of syringes. My tube is about 7 to 8 inches long and hangs out of a small hole they put in my stomach. It's connected to a small balloon that sits inside my stomach. The end of the tube has a cap on it that I keep closed when I'm not feeding. I flip it open when I start my feedings and connect the syringe into the end of the tube. I take the plunger out of the syringe and then pour 80ml of water into the syringe, holding it upright, to flush out the tube. Once the water works through the tube, I poor the Jevity from the can into the syringe. It takes about 25 to 30 minutes to get the whole can in. When I finish with the Jevity, I flush the tube out again with 80ml of water and cap the hole at end of the tube. That's it. Not too bad. Just looks a little odd. I did one feeding with Ann and one on my own before bed. I've got the hang of it.

I didn't feel good enough to go to work last night, so I stayed on the couch, watched tv and played poker online. I won $192 and went to bed. It's hard to believe that I'm not even finished with my chemo and radiation treatments. I hope the remaining ones don't make me sicker than I already feel. This is getting old fast!

TO BE CONTINUED....

Friends' Comments:

Jeffrey D.

Hi Jim, I have been following your journey and have to admit I have had difficulty finding the words to send. Your courage and determination are incredible, which is why I know we will be sipping gin martinis in the not too distant future. You are in my thoughts and prayers, Jim.

Karen/Mike Z.

Keep reminding yourself how fast time goes by. Already another month has passed. You're almost at the halfway mark and Fall has made its way past Summer. Wasn't it just June and July? And now we are approaching October already! I know it is so much easier said than done, but the time will continue to fly by and soon you will be at the 100% mark of treatments being finished. We continue to say prayers for you and keep you in our thoughts, cheering you on. You've got this one hands down! Keep winning at poker too. :)

John H.

Still hurling prayers and good karma your way, Jimmy!! Even though we can't be there, just remember that your friends and family are propping you up with their love and prayers from all over the country. You can do this!

Chapter 27

GREAT NIGHT AT ZING, TOUGH ONE FOR ME

Sept 20

IT RAINED ALL DAY. I decided to stay home on the couch and rest up so I could work tonight. We had a private dinner party for 48 scheduled on our garden patio with a band, plus we expected our usual busy Saturday night crowd. I've been trying to maintain a somewhat normal schedule, but it's becoming tougher and tougher to do as I get into the heart of my treatments. When I got to Zing at 5:45pm, we were already starting to seat guests... and it was pouring down rain. Of course it was! Fortunately, our two patios are covered by circus-type tents, so Scott had our servers and bussers doing their best to keep the tables moved far enough under the tent to keep them as dry as possible. Our band, Christy G & Velvet, had already set up and were also trying to stay dry. Scott wished upon the weather gods that the rain would stop and suddenly it did!

The sun came out, too. Phew...we would have had a mess on our hands had the rain continued.

Glad I had taken an Ativan before work, so I remained calm all evening. Scott did an amazing job tonight keeping the party organized and working with the kitchen to make sure everything was perfect. I'd be lost without him. His management of Zing is one less thing I have to worry about right now and I so appreciate that. We decided that I'd work with Bobbi at the host stand. It would give me a chance to greet folks, say hi, and let them know I'm doing as well as possible. It was nice to reconnect with a lot of friends and regulars, but I really wasn't feeling good. Since I can barely talk louder than a whisper, I was only able to chat briefly with folks. Bobbi handled all the incoming phone calls as I'm hard to understand when I do talk. It's definitely frustrating because generally I'm quite a chatterbox. My guess is by the end of next week, I won't want to be talking at all. It just hurts too much, even now. Not to mention that I can barely swallow my own saliva and collect it in my mouth until I find a place to spit it out.

As the evening went on, the smell of food started to make me nauseous. I had taken an anti-nausea pill before work, but it wasn't managing the issue well. I was also feeling tired after running around the restaurant for three hours, so I said my good-byes. Upon arriving home at 9:15pm, I had a splitting headache, painfully sore throat, and was feeling sick to my stomach. I immediately took a pain and anti-nausea pill and propped myself up on the couch wrapping a warm blanket around me. I turned on the Clemson vs. Florida State football game, fell asleep and woke up with Florida State winning in overtime 23-17. I'm watching Saturday Night Live now, but it's just not keeping me engaged. I'll check Facebook and go to bed. Hope tomorrow is a better day!

TO BE CONTINUED...

Friends' Comments:

Tammy W.
Jim, I'm really sorry to hear that the treatment is taking such a toll on you. I know it can be frustrating to have to slow down and not be able to do what you want or are used to doing. You are brave to share your story and I'm grateful that you are journaling and expressing yourself through this venue. The only encouragement I can offer up is that I'm still alive as a result of my treatment and, as bad as things get, it too will pass. Hang in there!

Donald M.

Jim, An author from Kalamazoo, Parker Palmer, wrote that all of us "should filter every thought through our hearts." You, my friend, are a perfect example. Our thoughts and prayers are with you. You are an inspiration to us all!

Dar W.

Hi Jimbo -- You know, you mention Scott so often in your posts. I don't know him, but he is a retaining wall. Angels are surrounding you, big guy. Praise God for that!

Chapter 28

In My Cave Today

Sept 21

I WOKE UP AT 7:45AM and rolled around in bed trying to get back to sleep, but couldn't. So I decided to pull myself together and go to church today, even though I could barely talk and felt like crap. I choked down a pain pill and did my "feeding" through the tube while watching the morning news. Each one takes a good 25 to 30 minutes, and I do it three times a day. It was windy and threatening rain, a perfect day to just lie on the couch. Once I "ate", and my pain pill kicked in, I felt a little better, took a shower and got dressed. Chris and Jodi picked me up at 9:45am. By 10am, the Douglas UCC was full of worshippers. The energy was contagious. I'm so glad to see this small little church doing so well. It's a real testament (no pun intended) to Pastor Sal, who I met with earlier this week. He makes everyone feel so good and welcome. "We are all ONE" is prominently displayed on the church program and elsewhere.

During the "Joys and Concerns" part of the service, members of the congregation openly share happy or good things that happened to them during the week and/or identify concerns or issues with themselves or others for which they desire prayer support. I was very touched when Rene asked the congregation to support ME with prayer, as I battle through my cancer treatments. It meant a lot. Next Sunday is a New Members Class from 12-2pm, so I'm looking forward to attending it. I understand that 22 or so people will be in the group.

After I got home from church, I gave myself another feeding and curled up on the couch for an afternoon of watching football and playing online poker. My throat was on fire, so I took a 15ml liquid version of my pain medication, Norco, and made myself sick. It just didn't sit well when it went down. I couldn't stop the nausea. Since there was nothing of substance in my system (except liquids), I got through it okay. Note to self...I need to regularly take my anti-nausea pill from Thursday night through Sunday, whether I think I'm going to be nauseous or not. Sometimes it just comes on out of nowhere. Once I recovered, I tried to take a nap, but wasn't successful. So I went with the original plan of watching football and playing online poker, covered myself with a blanket, and hung out in my "cave".

I needed the alone time to rest. I also caught up on Facebook, "whispered" with Chris on the phone, and did some reading. I tried something new and decided to put my liquid pain meds and Mucinex in my feeding tube, so I wouldn't have to swallow them. My docs told me I could do that, so I gave it a shot. They took effect extremely quickly. Nice!

My big accomplishment of the day was making scrambled eggs with small pieces of ham and cheese. I got most of it down, so was able to hit my caloric goal for the day. That was a first! I'll be watching the season premiere of "The Good Wife" tonight. It's one my favorite shows!

TO BE CONTINUED....

Friends' Comments:

Elizabeth B.

Hang in there, love! One more day until you get that infusion of steroids and a nice Benadryl nap. You are my hero, so brave! Thank you for sharing your journey. It helps us all keep things in perspective and realign priorities. Your healing and comfort are my priority, darling. Love you, xoxo

Duane M.
A day in "The Cave" never hurts. Hope all is well. Relax!

Chapter 29

Took a Fall, Jarred the Tube

Sept 22

I SLEPT ON AND OFF last night after going to bed at 11pm. At 3am, I woke up with a raging sore throat and a really bad phlegm drip, so I hooked up the syringe on my tube and fed myself liquid Norco and Mucinex. It worked fairly quickly, so I was back in bed by 3:20am and slept until 7:30am. I have a bowl on the bedside table with a Kleenex box next to it. Since I'm not able to swallow, I collect thick saliva in my mouth during the night and spit it out every couple of hours. There are usually five or six balls of Kleenex in the bowl that need to be dumped every morning. Really pleasant.

Elizabeth took me to radiation today. She did all of the talking during the car ride there, since it takes a lot of effort for me. I completed radiation treatment #15 of 35. This was the start of Week 4 of 7. It's painfully hard to believe that I still have a month of radiation treatments to get through... plus four more chemo treatments. The good news, however, is that I can tell the treatments are working! The lumps on both sides of my neck are significantly reduced in size.

After Elizabeth dropped me off at home, I gave myself my second feeding of the day and headed off to work to do some administrative stuff, pay bills and attend a meeting. It was an extremely slow business day at Zing, so I think this will be the last Monday we are open this year. I've also decided that, as of October 1, we'll only be open on Friday through

Sunday for the remainder of this year and Winter 2015. It's ridiculous how fast business drops off post-Labor Day Weekend.

I left the office at about 4:30pm and fell down a flight of ten stairs. I could see that I was going to crash headfirst into the cement wall at our main entrance, so I curled up during the free fall and held my breath. Luckily, I only suffered a couple of minor scrapes, a bruised left hip and a slightly twisted ankle. I felt like an idiot and hoped that no one saw me. Unfortunately, as I tumbled down the stairs, the feeding tube got yanked around a bit. Ironically, the hospital had just called earlier today to schedule stitch removal. Well, we don't need that appointment anymore. There was a little bleeding at the stoma (hole opening) and I noticed that the tube was more loose than usual.

I pulled myself together, drove to the bank and post office, and tried giving myself a feeding when I got home to see if I had damaged the tube or the inside of my stomach. I was a bit concerned when I was only able to get one syringe full of the canned liquid, Jevity, injected versus my usual three. I tried to cut off the second syringe, unsuccessfully. There was residual back up from my stomach pouring out of the tube on me. Since I forgot to immediately cover the hole at the bottom of the syringe, there was also canned liquid (think condensed milk) spurting out everywhere. It was a mess. I ran to the kitchen sink and started to get things under control.

Given that I was covered in liquid, I hopped in the shower to clean up. I then called the help line and described my problem. They told me to relax, tape everything down, and watch for bleeding. A consult is being scheduled for me tomorrow at Metro Health Hospital after I finish with chemo and radiation. I think all is okay with the tube, as I was able to do a normal feeding tonight without a problem. So the moral of this story is: "Don't fall down a flight of stairs with a feeding tube in your stomach."

TO BE CONTINUED....

Friends' Comments:

Star & Charlie
Our darling friend, be careful! Go slow. Let others help you. We love you.

Kat T.
We don't need a broken bone on top of your issues, mister! Thank goodness it wasn't worse.

John T.
Another example of your ability to bounce back. I think it is in your genes.

Duane M.
Oh Jim, I'm glad you didn't get seriously hurt. Be careful my friend, we don't need any broken bones at this point. Glad to hear things are shrinking, good news!

Chapter 30

A Long, But Good Day

Sept 23

CHRIS WORKED THE LATE SHIFT at the news last night and drove here to Douglas to see me. He arrived at about 12:15am. I was still a bit worked up from my fall, feeling achy, and hoping I hadn't damaged my feeding tube. Chris and I sat on the couch and watched tv while he rubbed my legs. It's always great being with him. I think we both needed to see each other last night. We're only able to get together every other weekend or so, and once during the week. My cancer has been hard on both of us, but we're managing. He always makes me feel good.

I woke up this morning at 8am and felt like I'd been run over by a Mack truck. I was sore down the left side of my body from the fall down the stairs and my left ankle was quite swollen. I had a slight fever and felt very flu-ish, so much so that I didn't even take a shower. I gave myself a feeding and threw on some sweats. Elizabeth picked me up at 9am and we headed to The Cancer Center. My throat was killing me, so Elizabeth did most of the talking. We mostly chatted about Business Association stuff and caught up on some personal things, too. She has been so wonderful through all of this and is an amazing friend.

I started off with my weekly blood tests, which looked good. Then, I went to hang out with "Henry", the linear accelerator (radiation machine), for our 16th session together. The rest of the time was spent at chemo, until about 3pm. My favorite part of the chemo treatment is the second bag of four. It has steroids and Benadryl in it. Generally, it puts me to sleep on most chemo days, especially if I come into it feeling tired. Today was no exception. It knocked me right out and I got a good one hour nap during the final two chemo bags. I woke up feeling refreshed, re-hydrated, and re-energized. The funny thing about chemo for me is that I feel really good immediately after it, and even better on Wednesday through mid-day on Thursday. However, starting on Thursday eve, I start to come off my temporary "high". Then, on Friday through Sunday, I fall into my chemo cave and generally feel miserable again until Tuesday. It's a vicious cycle.

Before we left The Cancer Center today, I did a photo shoot in my red, white and blue Speedo hooked up to my chemo IV apparatus. I showed a lot of skin, along with my hot looking feeding tube. Elizabeth and I got a good laugh. I needed to do something fun to lift my spirits and we thought others would get a kick out of it, too.

Upon leaving The Cancer Center, we drove over to Metro Health Hospital across the street and got my feeding tube checked out. A really nice male nurse cleaned it up and said that it looked like all was in good working order. I definitely lost an important stitch that was on the outside and inside of my stomach, but he thought the other stitch, while still intact, would do the job for now. I'll just need to keep an eye on it. When I got home, I gave myself a feeding and heated up some chicken noodle soup, which I was surprisingly able to eat. Just been resting tonight watching Dancing with the Stars, The Voice and Person of Interest. Time for another feeding. It was a long, but good day!

TO BE CONTINUED.....

Friends' Comments:

Charlene P.

So grateful it was a good day for you and thank goodness for Elizabeth and Chris, your angels, who obviously keep you positive and strong in fighting this disease. Praying for you each and every day!

Chapter 31
At the Halfway Point

Sept 24

I'M VERY RELIEVED THAT I'VE completed half of my treatments. My psychologist asked me today if what I've experienced so far is what I expected. I had no actual frame of reference going into this battle, so I had to think about my answer to his question. What I can say is that this certainly hasn't been easy, both physically and emotionally. Once I got over the shock, horror and sadness of being told that I had cancer, and was able to finally embrace it, I found the inner strength to deal with it. The support network around me, including all of you reading this journal, has been a huge asset to my emotional well-being. I've never felt alone on this journey. Your words of encouragement and inspiration keep me going, so thank you!

Physically, I've been tracking closely to what the doctors and nurses said I would experience. I started feeling sick around treatment #10, when they had projected treatment #12-15. They were right on with how sore my throat would be, the bad phlegm drip, the complete loss of taste and appetite, and the ongoing fatigue. I struggled with whether I should get the feeding tube or not, and they highly encouraged it. Repeatedly, they told me that the bi-lateral neck/base of tongue cancer patients have it the toughest, so I listened, heeded their advice and got the tube. I'm glad I did because there's absolutely no way I could ever consume 2500 calories a day, or even drink water, without it. It felt good yesterday when they told me that they're very happy with how I'm progressing so far.

Unfortunately, it sounds like my pain is going to get worse before it gets better (around end of Week 5/beginning of Week 6). I'm in mid-Week 4 now and I'm prepared to fight! An old high school friend, Patty, who has re-connected with me after over 35 years, has been full of thoughtful insights over the past few weeks. She writes, "I'm sorry to read that your treatments are getting the better of you. Remind yourself, when you're feeling your worst, that it's the drugs doing their job and it too shall pass. Don't be afraid to hunker down for the next couple of weeks. It's okay to just curl up on the couch, watch old movies, and sleep. You are not obligated to act like nothing is wrong. Pushing yourself is admirable, but taking care of yourself is critical. When you're tired and can't talk, that's your body's way of saying, "Cool it." So listen to your body." I plan to heed Patty's sage advice to get through the next month of treatments.

TO BE CONTINUED....

Friends' Comments:

Kristin A.

I continue to be amazed at not only your strength, Jim, but also your generosity. Sharing your journey is such a gift to the rest of us. Remarkable for those of us who have not been through cancer to better understand how it unfolds. And special, that we can know what you need and be there to help (as we can). Honestly, I'm sure you also know that humans WANT to help others.

I think we intuit that helping is a small way to try to shoulder some of the burden. It's truly a small way, but it's a signal that we want to be present to assist. So thank you for letting us be part of this and help, as we can and as you need it. Prayers, good thoughts, and hugs continue to come your way from our family to you!

Duane M.

You are at the top of the summit now heading down the hill to the end of the treatments and back to normal life. We are cheering for you and proud of your progress. One step at a time, you've got this beat.

Dan G.

"Hanging off a rock is an exaggerated experience of facing the unknown. It is exhilarating, scary, and completely vibrant. When we can't find a foothold, the mind falls into an open stillness, the same brief pause we encounter in any situation where we lose our familiar reference points. If we have the wherewithal to relax, we find our way."

- Elizabeth Mattis-Namgyel, "Open Stillness"

Chapter 32

FEELING ACCOMPLISHED

Sept 25

It's OFFICIAL! I'm over halfway done with my treatments. #18 of 35 radiation and #4 of 7 chemo sessions are in the books. I've climbed my way to the top of the hill and I see the finish line in the distance. It's definitely a marathon, not a sprint. I met with Dr. Julie today and I got a big "thumbs up" across the board. Feeling really good with my progress and can't wait for this to be over. I've got this covered!

TO BE CONTINUED....

Friends' Comments:

BJM
Good news, Jim. You are a trooper!

Josephine B.
YEAH!!! You are on the home stretch. We so admire your bravery. You are loved. Jodi and Chris

Donald M.
Fantastic! You are amazing. Your positive attitude is inspirational!

Charlene P.

Great attitude, Jim! Your strength and resolve will make the remainder of this journey a positive one with positive results. Xoxo

Chapter 33

Seems Like Cancer is Everywhere

Sept 26 & 27

CHRIS AND I WERE TALKING the other night about how we constant-
ly feel surrounded by the Big C because the media always seems to be
mentioning it. Seriously, test yourself on this. It feels like this ugly disease
is getting more than its fair share of exposure on tv, radio, billboards, news-
paper and social media. I wonder if it's because I'm battling cancer myself
and am just ultra sensitive to it or if, in fact, it's the season for it? The
next time you're in your car driving, or sitting at home watching tv, listen
and watch for all of the cancer-related talk show segments and cancer
treatment ads. Has it always been like this or have I just been shut off to
over the past few years? I can tell you that when I go for my daily radiation
treatments the waiting room is full with two or three patients and their
loved ones. It seems like we all know more than one person fighting cancer
for their life right now. How can this be? Why is it that this disease is
running rampant all over us? What has gone on in our lifetimes for us to
be at the point where everyone is susceptible? These are scary thoughts.
Everyone is a potential victim. No one is safe. Cancer doesn't discrimi-
nate. Where is the cancer prevention pill? We need one now! It's not right
that something so wrong has become a multi-billion dollar business. On
the positive side, cancer has created many jobs. And, more importantly,
with the advancement of technology and specialized doctors in the field,
cure rates are improving every day. This is highly encouraging and gives

me and others much needed hope. It just seems like cancer is everywhere. It needs to go away for good!

TO BE CONTINUED....

Friends' Comments:

John T.

The good part of this is the number of people I know who have been saved by all of the improvements in the science of cancer treatment! I know so many survivors. Thank goodness for the whole medical community.

Fran M.

Yes...it needs to go away. And you need to stay!!! Love surrounds you.

Tammy W.

It is everywhere and once you are diagnosed there are lots of people who make lots of money selling the equipment and treatments to "cure it." And then we must ask again, why is there no pill to prevent it? As a cancer survivor, who went through all the available medical treatment, I'm thankful to be alive and well. At the same time, we all need to look at the food we are eating (genetically modified and loaded with antibiotics or sprayed with pesticides), the air we are breathing, the drugs we are prescribed, and ask that question over and over again.

Chapter 34

FEELING REALLY SORRY FOR MYSELF

Sept 28

I'M HAVING A BAD WEEKEND. The weather is beautiful and I'm in my "chemo cave" feeling like crap. I was only able to work a couple of hours at Zing on Friday night before I was too tired to even stand up and had to go home. Plus, the smell of savory food makes me nauseous now, so that didn't help either. I stayed in all day Saturday and took a three hour nap hoping that I'd be able to work last night. Nope. That didn't happen. I feel that I've hit the proverbial wall at just over the halfway point of my treatments. I have absolutely no energy or desire to do anything except lay on the couch, watch tv and sleep in my bed. This is SO NOT ME. I'm always doing something. It's just all wrong. I can't eat, drink, swallow or taste anything. My throat is so sore. My mouth is constantly dry. I have thick, phlegmy, cement glue-like saliva that I want to spit out every chance I get. I have absolutely no appetite and now feed myself four times a day through the feeding tube. I have ongoing indigestion and am constipated. Nothing is normal.

Basically, this sucks! I'm trying to stay positive, but I'm exhausted. I'm so tired of being tired. I'm fed up with feeling like I have the flu every day. The only time I feel "good" (relatively speaking) is late Tuesday evening through Thursday night, after I've had my Tuesday chemo and the steroids are still active in my body. But when they wear off on Friday morning, I come crashing down over the weekend. I really wanted to go to church this morning and attend the New Members meeting from noon-2pm, but

I couldn't pull myself together. Today I feel like curling up in a ball and crying. It won't do me any good, but that's how it is. I just want all of this to be over, but I know I still have three weeks of chemo and radiation treatments to endure. Additionally, I'll have to get through at least four weeks of recovery, during which time I still won't feel good. I'm meeting with a palliative care doctor at The Cancer Center on Wednesday to see if there is some steroid-like medication that I can take to prevent falling into this chemo cave every week. I hope he has something in his bag of tricks. I'll take anything at this point. Sorry that I had to vent like this today, but I'm feeling really sorry for myself and just had to let it all out.

TO BE CONTINUED....

Friends' Comments:

Sharon L.
Nothing wrong with the way you are feeling. Lay down, curl up, watch tv, and cry. All is acceptable. You are not giving up or giving in. Your body is telling you that you need to rest and rebuild. I have admired your strength through all of this. I think you should turn your journal into a book. I am sure it will help others understand their fears and know to ask questions all the time, if they have them. I think you've done that well. Hunker down in your chemo cave for a little while. Then, get up and start again. You've come so far already. It can't be easy, but you can do it!

Doug G.
I say lie in a ball and cry. It does suck and you do feel crappy. It's okay to cry and let out all of those emotions. Hit a pillow! I know you. Once that's over, you will get your mojo back. I always feel so helpless in a situation like this. Wish the perfect words would come out to help but

1

your journey is so personal all I can say is take each day, hour or minute.. one at a time. You can and will do it.

Monty C.

Jim, it is healthy that you are being so open and honest about your journey with all of us who love and support you. I know you're feeling isolated. But don't forget that you are part of a special community that is lifting you up daily with prayers for increased strength and complete healing. You are loved by many. I hope you can draw courage and determination from that love to have victory over this cancer. We are all in this fight with you. xo

Charlene P.

Sorry you're feeling so sickly these days. This is when you really have to push through pain. Hope the palliative doctor will have some suggestions. I know you will get through this and that it will be difficult, but if anybody can do it you certainly can... and will!

Kristin A.

I don't think you're feeling sorry for yourself. I think you're feeling cancer. The fact that you write these wonderful posts is more proof that you are ahead and pulling away. This too shall pass my friend. Deep breath, another nap, and watch the days tick away. Soon enough you'll be looking forward to that cruise you want to take at the end of November. Hugs and more hugs.

Dar W.

CANCER does not play fair but you, big guy, will beat it regardless. Your choice to see a palliative care doctor just proves that you are doing all you need to do to stay on top of this, and beat the heck out of this horrible thing. Prayers are being sent to lessen the pain and your stress. Hugs!

Mary Kay B.

Jim, that's what friends are for...listening to you vent. This whole process is awful but continue to know that each and every day you are one step closer to restored health! Thanks for being honest and letting us all share the load for you.

Paula H.

You are telling it like it is. Of course, you are going to have some miserable times because this is a miserable disease that you're fighting. But you ARE still fighting and that's what matters. One day at a time.

BJM

Hey Jim, you deserve to be depressed and vent your feelings. It does suck. It sucks! It sucks! IT SUCKS! I'll scream it for you. I think your idea about getting help from the palliative doctor, so your weekends aren't so F'ing horrible, is brilliant and positive. Go for it!

Chapter 35

Napping is my Best Friend

Sept 29

I've been going to bed around 10:30 to 11pm each night and usually wake up at 3am when my body decides it wants a feeding, needs water, or craves pain meds. It's sort of like having a baby that must be attended to. Last night was no different. I got out of bed, threw myself on the couch, and watched ABC News' World NOW from 3 to 4am. I moved to my "feeding chair" and and started to get drowsy. Upon drifting off for the third time, I pulled myself out of the chair and got back into bed.

I woke up at 8am and gave myself another feeding. Then I showered, shaved, and got dressed. I've started losing the hair on my face. I saw that it was getting "patchy" the other day and last night I noticed small silver gray hairs all over my black sweat shirt. Yep, that's one of chemo's side effects. Looks like I'll be wearing the clean shaven look for awhile now.

Elizabeth picked me up and took me to radiation. I finished #20 of 35 treatments today. I was really tired on both the ride up and back to The Cancer Center. When I got home, I went right back to bed for a 90 minute nap. When I awoke, I gave myself a feeding, got dressed and went to work for three hours. I had a lot of administrative stuff to do, which has been weighing on my mind, so it felt good to get that done. My energy ran out, so I came home and got in bed again for a two hour nap. This is my new strategy for dealing with "bad" days. I'm just going to get as much sleep as I can through napping!

TO BE CONTINUED....

Friends' Comments:

Brian C.
Good approach, Jim! Take those naps. Your body is sending you a message loud and clear.

John T.
I'm watching Joan Lunden speak about her cancer. I hope you realize how much people like me appreciate all that you and others like her are sharing about this awful disease. We all worry about someday having cancer ourselves. Knowing it IS possible to tough through treatment like you're doing, makes the notion of going through treatment seem possible - not easy- but possible. Thanks!

Chapter 36

More of the Same

Sept 30 & Oct 1

FATIGUE, BODY ACHES AND BAD sore throat continue. Nothing new to report. Completed treatments #5 of chemo and #22 of radiation. I'm counting down the days to October 20, my last treatment day. I still have 19 days to go. Seems daunting. The end can't get here soon enough. Chris just arrived and he'll lift my spirits. It's Day 1 of Breast Cancer Month. I'm really pleased to see how Joan Lunden has come forth with her story and is inspiring so many. I watched her on Good Morning America today and was so impressed. She will help so many.

TO BE CONTINUED....

Friends' Comments:

Donald M.

You put a whole new meaning to the words tough and resilient. Your ability to be resourceful and self-sufficient reaches new heights each day of your journey. As you traverse through the wilderness toward completing your chemo and radiation treatments, know that you are an inspiration to all who know you. October 20th will be a true day of celebration!

Kristin A.

I was thinking the other day about your situation and how hard it is to be wading through something. Even when you know there is an end date, knowing it does nothing to make you feel better on that day. But, knowing there is an end date does give hope and a certain knowledge that the current situation is temporary. Painful, exhausting, depressing, angering ... but ultimately GONE. Done. Finished. Behind you. No more. And then you begin the joyful healing journey, which you have actually started. But now the journey is more about shedding and sloughing. Soon it will be about regaining and rebuilding. For now, sleep. Know that the days ARE numbered. We will all raise a glass to you on October 20!

Ed B.

Jim, we ache with you and are lifted by your endurance and vulnerability. We continue to keep you in our thoughts and prayers.

BJM

Hang in there. One day this will all be a bad memory.

Chapter 37

I Can Do This!

Oct 2 & 3

I'VE BEEN IN TREATMENT FOR five weeks, receiving radiation daily and chemo weekly. I have eleven radiation and two chemo treatments to go.

I met yesterday with my doctors and they are really pleased with my progress so far. The neck tumors have significantly reduced in size and they're very optimistic that the base of tongue tumor (my primary cancer site) is responding similarly, although they cannot see or feel it. I was "reprimanded" for losing weight over the past week (about 12 pounds overall), especially since I'm feeding myself through the tube. I haven't eaten real food in three weeks. It tastes horrible and feels like broken glass ripping into the lining of my throat when I swallow. I've been averaging about four cans per day of the protein and nutrient-rich, Jevity. But the docs really want me to be consuming five to six cans of it, so that my caloric intake is between 2000 to 2500 calories given my size and weight. So, I either need to feed myself one can five times a day or increase my four feedings to 1.25 to 1.5 cans each. ARGH. Each feeding takes about 45 minutes, so I have to be sure I schedule them into my day. I've also been put on an additional steroid-type pain medication, which should help regulate my post-chemo lows when I bottom out during the weekends.

I went to work for a couple of hours after radiation today, but quickly got tired and went home to take my daily two hour nap. Since we're going to be very busy tomorrow night at Zing, and also have two offsite catering functions, I decided to stay home tonight and rest up so I'm ready to pitch in and help tomorrow.

Chris worked the afternoon shift at the news station until 11:15pm and is on his way here now to spend the weekend. It will be so nice to get some quality time with him. It has been a couple of weeks since we've been able to do that. I hope I'm feeling better than usual and that we can go to a movie on Sunday. I really want to see Gone Girl with Ben Affleck. I'm 2/3's of the way done with treatments with two weeks to go. I can and will get this done! My goal is to be on a November 30th cruise out of Fort Lauderdale with my angel and friend, Scott. I bought the cruise for him as a surprise 50th birthday gift, before I was diagnosed with my cancer. Today, we booked our airline tickets for the trip. I'll have from October 21 (day after my last treatment) to November 27 to get myself "cruise-ready". I don't want to let him or myself down, so I WILL be on that cruise!

TO BE CONTINUED....

Friends' Comments:

Dar W.
You may not know this, but your journey is an inspiration to those of us out here. So cruise away, big guy.

Duane M.
You've got this Jim, keep it going!

Chapter 38

BEST WEEKEND IN FIVE WEEKS!

Oct 4 & 5

I RESTED ALL DAY YESTERDAY so I could work at Zing last night. We had two offsite catering functions that Scott was managing, so I really needed to be at the restaurant for what would be a very busy Saturday night. The stars aligned and for once I didn't feel too sick on a Saturday night. I was prescribed new, steroid-based pain meds this week to help me get through the weekends, which generally have been very tough for me since initiating treatments five weeks ago. Thankfully, they kicked in and did the job! I was able to host and manage from 6 to 9:45pm. It felt really good. I was especially happy that Chris was there to help me too, as we've been short a host since the end of September. He has consistently been there for me when he can be. I'm so glad that he came into my life three weeks before all this cancer craziness started. I always look forward to his visits. He lifts me up when I'm feeling down, and there has been a lot of that.

This morning we went to church at the Douglas Congregational UCC. I was one of 34 new members inducted, which was about one-third of the congregation in attendance today. I feel so spiritually at home there and find Pastor Sal's homilies to be energizing, relevant, and real. I'm glad I was encouraged by my friends, Jodi & Chris, to start joining them at church about a month ago. I know it's going to make a big difference in my life now. For many years, I have felt a bit incomplete without it and know that regularly attending church is going to stimulate a spiritual re-awakening for me.

Since I've been having a good day, Chris and I decided to take advantage of that and went to see Gone Girl, the new psycho-thriller starring

Ben Affleck. It was twisted, odd, disturbing, and at times, unbelievable, but was definitely entertaining and worth seeing. Neither of us were satisfied with the ending. It left too many unanswered questions, but did leave room for a sequel. Chris is at the gym now and I'm watching the SF vs. KC football game. I have a chance to win this week's football pool if KC can score and win the game in the last four minutes, but they just made a huge, stupid error by having too many men on the field. Oh well. Really looking forward to spending the rest of the evening with Chris watching Madame Secretary, The Good Wife, and Revenge, one of our favorite tv shows. It has been a great weekend! I really needed it. It has given me much needed energy to get through my last two weeks of treatments.

TO BE CONTINUED....

Friends' Comments:

Mary Kay B.
It was such fun to read about your weekend. You can hear the energy in your words. What a blessing to have found and now become a member at Douglas UCC. Sal is helping them grow like crazy - how great! I saw the movie on Friday and completely agree with your assessment. The book ended the same way. I continue to pray for 100% healing and the energy and stamina to get through the rest of your treatments. You are getting much closer!

Charlene P.
Great! The new meds are allowing you to feel better and that's definitely a step in the right direction. So glad Chris was there for you. Take care and stay strong. Keeping you in my prayers. Xoxo

Lee S.
You are almost there. The finish line is within sight!

Chapter 39

TIME TO TALK ABOUT SEX AND CANCER

Oct 7

I'VE BEEN STRUGGLING ABOUT WHETHER to journal about how cancer is affecting my sex life. I'm not known for being shy or holding back, so I'm going to dive into this topic with honesty and candor because it's a reality that can't be avoided when one is battling the Big C. Interestingly, while in college at Cornell University (MANY years ago), I was a teaching assistant for a Human Sexuality class, so discussing sex comes pretty easy for me. This is your warning to not read on if you think this journal entry might get uncomfortable for you. Of course, I will do my best to appropriately handle the topic.

I will be the first to admit that sex is very important to me on many levels. It's more than one dimensional. Yes, there is the amazing, physical, "feel good" sensation we get before, during and after sex, whether it's oral or intercourse sex. But for GREAT sex, there need to be the facets of trust, intimacy, sensuality, and if we're really fortunate, love. For me, touching also plays a critical role across the board. Don't get me wrong, I do love the intense physicality of sex, but it's so much better when the emotional and spiritual elements are woven in to make the whole experience greater than the sum of its parts.

I've got to tell you that Cancer knows how to mess with your mind, body, and soul in so many ways. The first time you're told you have it, you can't believe you're hearing the words. You immediately jump to "People with cancer die, so there's a good chance I might die." Then you wrestle with the questions: "Why me?, How did this happen?, What did I do to deserve this?, How could I have prevented it from happening to me?, Will I ever be the same?, How sick am I going to get?, Am I going to die?, How will I get through this? Who will be there for me?, Will anyone want me?", along with a host of other unpleasant thoughts. You're immediately put on anti-depression, anti-anxiety, anti-nausea, and anti-pain meds, all while having to travel 70 miles daily to receive 35 intensive radiation and seven body-racking chemo treatments.

So where does Sex play in all of this? Absolutely nowhere right now. How could it?! And, that's just killing me because I'm such a sexual person and enjoy it so much. The ironic, and sad fact of the matter is, I hardly ever think about sex anymore. My body and mind have been brutally invaded by both this debilitating, horrible disease AND the resulting after effects of my treatments and meds.

I have ongoing fatigue, daily flu-like symptoms, an unbearable sore throat, tons of pain, and many of the worries outlined above. I haven't had real food or anything to drink (other than water for pills) through my mouth in over three weeks. I feed myself four times (four hours) a day through a tube inserted in my stomach. And, I have to continue with that for at least another four or five weeks. I have constant phlegm drip, no taste buds, and a constant pool of nasty, thick saliva in my mouth that I have to spit out or choke down. I wake up in the morning with crusty lips and horrible bad breath. Why am I telling you this? Because this is my reality and the reality for others who are sick like me. It's so hard to not be in complete control of your physical and emotional state when battling cancer. All you can do is what you can do at the moment, while following doctors' orders and trying to remain positive.

When it comes to Sex, it's almost an unimaginable concept. This is quite difficult to comprehend and accept. I don't feel handsome, sexy, sensual, desirable, interesting, appealing or fun. I just feel "Blah". I give so much credit to Chris. He has stuck with me this entire time and makes me feel good just by being in the same room with me. We've only known each other for four months, but have grown very close. Relationships truly get tested when things aren't all hunky dory and obstacles present themselves. That's how it has been for us. He is seeing me at my absolute worse and I'm getting to know him for the man he is.

Although our physical sex life has significantly dwindled over the past six weeks (all do to me), the intimacy we've experienced together has helped keep me going in so many ways. It's amazing what touching someone else can do. Please touch your husband, wife, partner, kids, friends, and loved ones in a caring way whenever it feels right. I just can't put into words how good it feels when Chris rubs my feet, legs, and head. It's a way to be close to one another, that is intimate, caring, and refreshing, with no pressure or expectation that the physical act of sex must come next. We're both snugglers in bed, too. Taking turns holding one another and wrapping ourselves up in each other arms feels so right. I'm starting to see now why my therapist has been pushing me a bit on the concept that developing intimacy, and truly caring about someone from the inside out, should lead to a more fulfilling sex life and enduring long term relationship. I'm excited to explore this more. Perhaps this will be one of my important gifts from Cancer when all is said is done?!

Friends' Comments:

Doug G.
Very raw and honest, Jim. Thank you sharing and helping us to understand a glimpse of your journey.

Chris F.
You are an awesome man! I'm glad I am able to help you through all of this. Your strength inspires me and so many others. Two more weeks and this will be behind you!

Dan G.

Jim, that was a brave and courageous share. Your fearlessness and fierceness with talking about cancer is inspiring and revealing. Hang in there. You continue to amaze me. So glad you have Chris with you.

Lauren F.

Ok, don't kill me Jim, but you're starting to sound like a lesbian! :) Seriously, thanks for your authentic sharing. I so admire you and am 100% in your corner. I had some serious health issues in my youth, and my grandma always told me "What doesn't kill me will make me strong." I used to nod my head, but it is true. The man you are becoming is the best you yet. And it will get better. xoxo

Charlene P.

So touching and heartfelt that you shared your feelings about all that you're going through. Brave, honest and beautiful. Thank you. You can and will get through this. I just know it!

Chapter 40

Finally, In the Home Stretch

Oct 8 & 9

IT'S AMAZING HOW THE BODY works and responds to chemicals, both good and bad. For the past six weeks, Wednesday has been my best day of the week. This is the result of some really great steroids that get pumped into me during the chemo infusion process every Tuesday. They provide a wonderful, but very temporary, false high for a couple of days, while alleviating a lot of the soreness in my throat and providing a much needed kick start of energy.

Yesterday was awesome. I woke up early, had a feeding, drove myself to radiation, stopped by the restaurant for an hour, had a 90 minute eye doctor appointment, went to the bank and post office, attended a meeting at my new church, and returned to the restaurant to work in the office for a couple of hours. It was a productive day. I actually felt normal for a change! So refreshing. And then, today rolled in and hit me like a brick.

After a decent night's sleep, I woke up extremely queasy with an ex- cruciating sore throat and overall fatigue. I dragged myself out of bed and headed for my row of pill bottles on the bathroom counter. It's quite a sight and looks like I have my own pharmacy. This morning I took everything: anti-nausea, anti-pain (two different ones), anti-anxiety, anti-depression, and anti-acidity. It's always a big undertaking as I can barely swallow, so I have to psyche myself up to gag down the pills. It takes about five minutes to get them all down. I could pulverize them and put them in my feeding tube, but that's just too much work. Plus, it's recommended that I swallow something each day, even if it hurts, so I don't lose the reflex. So much fun.

I texted Scott to see if he would take me to radiation today. I was feeling nauseous and just wasn't up for driving solo 70 miles in my sickly state. Scott picked me up and we made the daily journey. It's official! I only have seven more radiation treatments to go. I'm 80% DONE (28 of 35 completed) and only have one more chemo treatment left to endure on next Tuesday. I can see the finish line and am in the home stretch!

We met with Dr. Julie, my radiation oncologist, and she was very encouraging about my progress. However, she did mention that the last week and a half of treatments may be a bit unpleasant given her experience with other patients. I've gotten this far, so I know I can gut it out eleven more days to October 20th. The docs and nurses have been on me a bit about my weight, so I'm pleased to say that I maintained it for the week at 219 lbs (down from 230 lbs when treatments started). They're highly suggesting that I eat and drink more through my mouth, but it's just too difficult right now. Everything tastes so bad or has absolutely no taste, and hurts too much going down my throat. That's why I'm relying totally on the feeding tube. I'll need to start weaning myself off of it once treatments stop, so I can prove to them (and myself) that I can eat enough on my own to maintain my weight without the tube. I don't want this tube sticking out of me when I go on the cruise with Scott at the end of November, so I've got some work to do. After Scott dropped me off at home, I went right to my bedroom, threw myself on the bed and slept for 2 1/2 hours. I've had zero energy today. Very frustrating, but somewhat expected. At least I know the end is in sight.

TO BE CONTINUED....

Friends' Comments:

Lauren F.

You're doing very well, all things considered. Of course, saying that doesn't give you back the well-being and energy you seek, but hopefully the perspective is helpful. You are so strong and so positive, and you are truly on the home stretch. Hold those thoughts and you will make it through. You are an amazing man, sending you lots of XOXOXO

Fran M.

You are such an inspiration. You are amazing. Thank you for sharing your journey. All of us have been with you, are with you, and will be with you at the finish line. God Bless you, Jim. Peace and love be with you.

Karen/Mike Z.

I'm hearing the theme song from the original Rocky movie playing now for you.

You're a champ. You are fighting and winning!

Chapter 41
YOU Inspire Me

Oct 13

HI FRIENDS. THIS IS MY 41st journal entry on CaringBridge.org. I can't believe that I've had over 2,000 total site visits in just two months. You have no idea how helpful and reassuring it is to know that you are all behind me, pushing me forward, and keeping me going. I've "hit the wall" a few times along the way, but each evening, when I read your comments and feel your prayers, YOU give me renewed energy. I don't feel alone in my battle. It would just be too much to handle alone. You've collectively become my fifth angel (my "Circle of Friends"), joining Elizabeth, Scott, Chris and Dr. Julie F. Although I don't respond individually to most of your comments, I definitely do read and process each and every one. Please keep them coming. You all inspire me so much! Thanks for being there for me.

TO BE CONTINUED....

Friends' Comments:

Dar W.
A two-way street it seems. Hugs, big guy.

John H.

It is your strength and determination that inspire all of us to face our own daily struggles and challenges, physical or otherwise. Hang in there, my dear. xoxox

Donald M.

Jim, it is you, my friend, that is the inspiration. Your openness has helped each one of us understand and refocus on what is really important in life. You are in the final few laps of a courageous journey. The checkered flag is about to be waved and we will all be celebrating not only your victory lap but your life.

Ally and Don

Jeanne S.

You inspire US Jim, thank you for sharing your journey. After going through my sister's journey and inevitable loss, you don't realize how your words echo my sister's, yet I feel you are going to win your battle. Keep fighting!

Josephine B.

You are in our hearts and prayers. Your courage encourages us. Thank you for receiving our (everyone's) love with open arms. You are on the home stretch!

Chapter 43

SEEING THE LIGHT

Oct 16

I FINISHED MY LAST CHEMO infusion yesterday and have just three more radiation treatments to go. It has been a long 6 1/2 week haul, but I'm finally seeing the light at the end of this dark tunnel.

In other good news today, Scott will be released from Holland Hospital tomorrow where he has been in treatment for almost a week now with a ruptured colon. The intensive antibiotics he received cleared up his massive diverticulitis infection to the point where major colon surgery is not needed at this time. I'm so glad I got him to the doctor before this became a fatal problem. If you have something odd going on with your body, like an unusual lump, mole or pains, DON'T WAIT to get it checked out. Go immediately to your doctor and get the evaluation process started. The sooner you catch it, the better chance it has of being addressed and corrected... and very possibly, saving your life. Don't try to be a hero and tough it out.

Overall, I'm feeling pretty good. That's usually the case on Wednesday after my Tuesday chemo treatment. One of the bags of fluid I get at each infusion has great steroids which helps take a lot my pain away and gives me a nice burst of energy, usually through Thursday evening. Then I hit bottom, on Friday through Monday, when the chemo cave hits and I feel really sick again. This weekend should be the LAST time I experience the cave as chemo is now officially done! Hopefully, some of my new pain meds will help make this weekend be more manageable, too. Elizabeth, one of my angels, took me to chemo/radiation yesterday and radiation today. She has taken such great care of me and is an amazing friend! She brought a bouquet of roses for us to distribute to my team of nurses. The girls loved them. I also gave my primary chemo nurse, Jessica, a candle as a special "Thank you". The staff at Metro Health's Cancer Center has been absolutely wonderful. I highly recommend them. Elizabeth is so thoughtful. She also gave me a "You're Awesome" helium balloon and a beautiful dragon fly wind chime as Chemo Graduation gifts. And so we celebrated!

On the way to radiation this morning, we chatted about how people come in and out of your lives when you least expect it and/or for a reason. This is not coincidental. It's meant to be. We both believe that a higher power has laid out a path for our respective lives. The path includes peaks, valleys, obstacles, detours and choices all along the way. We will end up where we are supposed to be, but as a more evolved, enriched, emotional, empathetic, loving, nurturing, and humbled individual because of the vast set of life experiences (good and bad) that we will live through as we advance along our personal pathway.

I know Saugatuck-Douglas is where I'm supposed to be right now in my life. My higher power wanted me to be in a place where my angels could reach out and touch me, and where a caring community would unselfishly embrace and support me during my battle with cancer. With tears in my eyes, I told Elizabeth how glad I am that she came into my life. I feel so blessed to have her as my friend. I know she would do anything for me, as I would for her. I am seeing the light now in so many ways.

TO BE CONTINUED....

Friends' comments:

Dar W.

Jim, what a tremendous acknowledgment you offer of how people care for each other. You do indeed have angels and, frankly, you are one as well. Scott feels that I bet, and with the abundance of nurturing coming from Elizabeth, it's she that secretly thanks you. Only a few more treatments and you're on the mend, big guy.

John H.

Jim, your words about your Higher Power are spot on. I no longer believe in coincidences! Everything that happens in my life is part of God's plan for me, which is revealed to me on HIS timeline, not mine. I'm so happy for you in finishing chemo. You have been such a role model to all of us who have yet to face such life-threatening circumstances. I'm so proud of you! Thoughts and prayers still coming your way.

Marilyn B.

Blessings to you and all of your angels, Jim.

Chapter 44

Did What I Love Today

Oct 16 & 17

FOR ALMOST SEVEN WEEKS NOW, I feel like I've been living in a cage. With a regimented daily schedule including radiation treatments, the need for constant rest, and four daily feedings through my tube, I haven't been able to do or get out much. It has really been tough just hanging out at home on my couch or in my bed, being totally unproductive. I have missed the stimulation of regular "everyday life". Wow, I never thought I'd be saying that!

I woke up yesterday with a lot of energy and decided that if all went well at radiation, I would do something fun for a change. Many of you may know that I play poker professionally part-time. I've had a good run this year, especially this past June, and have been wanting so badly to get back to the tournament circuit. So I decided to drive myself to Battle Creek, MI to play in the Mid States Poker Tour Main Event at Firekeepers Casino. This is a fairly large regional event with a guaranteed prize pool of at least $200K. I believe this year's pool will be over $400K. There are three starting days on which you can begin play. I chose the Thursday 4pm group because I need to work on Friday and Saturday nights at Zing this weekend. Everyone in the tourney pays $1,110 for their entry. My group (Day 1A) had 122 entrants and after 14 levels of 40-minute play there were 23 of us remaining with chips. We all now advance to Day

2 on Sunday morning with the chip stacks we accumulated. The good news is that we started with 20K in chips and I have 148K going into Day 2, which puts me in the top 10 players of my qualifying group. It's very tough playing for 10 hours from 4pm-2am with only ten minute breaks every two hours, but I did it. I played smart and solid, even though I started feeling pretty sick around 10pm. I'm now in great position to make some good money on Sunday, when my qualifying group will be joined with today's and tomorrow's qualifying groups to play for the championship. It felt so good to engage in what I LOVE to do for a change...and to get out of my cage.

I booked a room at the Quality Inn next to Firekeepers, stayed the night, and drove myself to radiation this morning from there. It was a beautiful drive. I took in all of the colors and was excited to know that today would be my second to last radiation treatment (#34 of 35). Yes, one more to go on Monday and I'm DONE! Then I have a three-month recovery period before I can have a PET Scan to see if all of the cancer is gone. I've got this. I see the finish line. I'm going to win! Off to work now for a couple of hours.

TO BE CONTINUED....

Friends' Comments:

Tammy W.
Great news! You're such an inspiration and a WINNER in several ways! Wish you well.

Donald M.
You are crossing the finish line with all of us exuberantly cheering!

Patti T.

Jim, I always knew you would win. It's so beautiful to see you being able to put everything you're going through aside and take a moment for yourself. You are amazing. Best wishes always.

Chapter 45

So Nauseous Tonight

Oct 18

I WAS REALLY HOPING TO have a good night at work and not get sick. Unfortunately, that wasn't the case. Given that I have no taste buds and can't even taste Listerine mouthwash or Colgate toothpaste, my sense of smell has taken over. One of the chemo side effects is nausea and I've been doing pretty well with it until the past couple of weekends. Last night, the smell of buttered popcorn did me in. Tonight, it was our salmon. I really wanted to be at Zing for the entire evening, as we had both a wedding dinner for 18 and a 50th birthday/engagement party for 24... plus our usual Saturday crowd. I only lasted 1 hour 45 minutes.

I'm so glad that my chemo treatments have ended. Hopefully, this will be the last time I have nausea because it isn't fun. It absolutely kills my already beat up throat when I'm gagging. Not a pleasant experience. I also wanted to stop into the Make A Wish fundraiser at The Dunes Resort across the street tonight. It's always a great event and for a such a wonderful cause, but I'm home now on the couch trying to relax. Looks like I'll catch the second half of the Notre Dame vs. Florida State game. I can't believe I'm going to say this, but "GO ND"!

On my way out of the restaurant tonight, after my third episode of nausea, I saw the partner of the 50th Birthday "boy" standing at the head of his table of 24. He was reading off three handwritten sheets proclaiming how much he loves his partner and admires him for how he has handled his personal battle with HIV/AIDS and other health issues over the years...

NEVER giving up! It was an amazing public testament in front of their closest friends and family members. I was so touched by the beauty of his words, his confidence in expressing his true feelings, and the energy he showed in his delivery. It almost made me cry. These two gentlemen have been through "thick and thin" with each other. They've had their highs and some very low lows, but have endured it all because of their strength, love for each other, and maintenance of a positive attitude, even in the most dire situations.

I can really relate to trying to keep a positive attitude. It has been an awful seven weeks for me, but I've tried to see myself on the other side of it all. My cancer is a big obstacle that I've learned to deal with. I did not let it bring me down. Instead, I made the conscious decision to fight the fight, remain as positive as possible, and know in my heart that this too shall pass. I've surrounded myself with positive people and energizing situations when I can. I am so looking forward to being done with all of my treatments on Monday and not having this bullshit nausea anymore.

TO BE CONTINUED....

Friends' Comments:

Donald M.
Our thoughts and hearts continue to surround you. Each day brings you closer to concluding this incredible journey. Your ability to remain positive is felt by all of us.

Elizabeth B.
Hi Baby! So sorry you have had to endure the discomfort and unpredictability of the nausea. You have put up an excellent fight and I am so grateful to be part of your journey to health and cancer free living! You are almost there. I have looked forward to "Tuesdays with Jim" and the

laughs and closeness we share. You are my hero! You have walked through this crisis with dignity and grace. We can all learn a lesson from your perseverance and positivity. Love you, Sweetheart. Big hugs and kisses XOXOXOXO

Cory R.

Hi Jim. I love your last two posts! We are also on the couch watching ND and Florida St. Choosing between the two is difficult as we hate both teams. MSU beat IND today and they are now 6-1, so you know who is very happy. We are so excited that you played some great poker and did something you love for once. I'm thinking this will be your last and final bout of nausea EVER. Congrats on nearly being done with everything. You are SO STRONG AND AMAZING and we are really proud of you. Your inspirational journals have helped me get through the last eight weeks of my own battle. I sustained a bad concussion (my sixth) and now have post-concussion syndrome. I've spent the last eight weeks in bed, in the dark and quiet, with many of the same symptoms you have. Your wonderful words have helped me keep a positive attitude despite being sequestered in a brain healing mode. So thank you for that! I too am finally starting to emerge from the cocoon and am seeing progress. I wish for you a cancer-free body and future! All our love, always and forever. Go Florida State!

Chapter 46

CASHED IN THE POKER TOURNEY!

Oct 19

I GOT UP EARLY THIS morning, fed myself two cans of Jevity in my feeding tube, and was on the road at 8:15am to Firekeepers Casino in Battle Creek. It was 30 degrees outside, so my car was frosted over and I had to scrape it first. The 1 hour 20 minute drive was absolutely beautiful with the trees baring their peak Fall colors. Today was Day 2 of the Main Event in the Mid-States Poker Tour. I qualified on Thursday after playing ten hours and accumulating 148K in chips from a starting stack of 20K. On Friday and Saturday, 97 other players made it through to Day 2. Overall, there were a total of 517 players in the tournament and I began today in 21st place among the 98 remaining players. Only the top 54 would each earn a minimum of $2K, so I had to outlast at least 44 players. GOOD NEWS is that I placed 23rd overall for $2,750. Given how sick I've been feeling (I only threw up once today), I'm really pleased with how I played and am excited to have cashed. I feel like my juju is back and I that I'm slowly getting on track again! Tomorrow is my LAST radiation treatment. Hopefully, I'll gradually start feeling better soon. Thanks for all of your good thoughts and wishes. Please keep them coming. I still have a lot of recovery to get through.

TO BE CONTINUED....

Friend's Comments:

Marlys J.

Hi Jim! Thanks for sharing your site. You have a wonderful testimony. It was our pleasure to meet you at Dave's on Saturday night. We will continue to pray for your full recovery and strength for each new day. A hug to you!

Annette C.

You are truly a force of nature.

Tammy W.

Congratulations on coming in 23rd overall! Jim, I'm totally in awe of your tenacity and ability to share your journey. You will start feeling better before you know it. Safe travels tomorrow and a make sure you say a pleasant goodbye to your Jason mask, mouth guards, and your team of radiologists!

Chapter 47

Treatments are DONE!

Oct 20

I CAN'T BEGIN TO TELL you how happy I am that all of my chemo (7) and radiation (35) treatments are now done! It has been a VERY LONG seven weeks. I decided to go alone today, as I just sort of needed to process everything on my own. Upon arriving, I had my final weigh-in and put up 210 lbs on the scale for a total weight loss during treatments of about 19 lbs, which isn't too bad at all. I will continue "eating and drinking" through the feeding tube for another three weeks or so, as my throat will be very sore for the next few weeks while the radiation continues to work. I will also be taking all of my pain medications until I don't need them anymore.

After my final radiation blast today, I thanked all of the technicians and nurses for taking such good care of me. They were so awesome. I was given a graduation certificate that was signed by everyone and then was presented with my Green Hornet/Jason radiation mask. I'm not sure what I'm going to do with it yet. It may be part of my Halloween costume for this coming weekend's festivities or I may just burn it at a bonfire sometime.

Please keep your prayers and good thoughts coming as I still have quite the healing process to get through. I have to believe that my treatments have worked as designed and, in turn, kicked my cancer's ass. Unfortunately, we won't know for sure until January 20 (three months from now) when I will have a PET scan to see if the cancer is completely gone. It just has to be!

So as a little reward for myself today, I decided to drive to the Horseshoe Casino in Hammond, IN to play in the World Series of Poker Circuit events being held there. I didn't fare well, but had a great time and am staying tonight at the Ameristar Casino Hotel, which is surprisingly very nice! I'm not sure if I'll play more poker tomorrow or just get on the road back to Douglas. I'll see how I feel in the morning. I will sleep well tonight knowing that I don't have to go to radiation and chemo tomorrow...or hopefully, ever again!

TO BE CONTINUED....

Friends' Comments:

Fran M.
We know you will keep moving forward. Do so swiftly. Your friends have your back! Sending continued prayer, renewed peace, and love. Today is your first day of Spring.

Josephine B.
Jim, we are so happy that the treatments are over! We will continue to keep you in our prayers. You have been such an inspiration for everyone and as brave as a lion. Wow. Let's celebrate!

Marilyn B.
AMEN!

Monty C.
Jim, there is light at the end of the tunnel! We have been inspired that you have gone through this experience with such grace and courage. By sharing your journey with those of us who call you friend, it is obvious that

you have emerged a stronger, better man. Sending prayers for continued healing. Much love.

Duane M.

So glad for you, Jim, that it's behind you. Thank you for keeping us all posted throughout the process. Our prayers continue for your full recovery. You are a Saint!

Donald M.

As your healing continues, the numerous seeds planted by you grow within each of us... internalizing the meaning of understanding, care, love, compassion to name a few. You sharing your journey has made an incredible impact on each of us. Thank you!

Gerrie B.

Now the real healing can begin! Every day stronger.

Chapter 48

PLAYED SOME MORE POKER THIS WEEK

Oct 21-23

GIVEN THAT I CASHED IN the Mid-States Poker Tour Main Event on Sunday in Battle Creek and finished all of my cancer treatments on Monday, I decided to treat myself to a mini poker vacation. The World Series of Poker Circuit event is currently at the Horseshoe Casino in Hammond, IN, so I drove there on Monday after my final radiation treatment. I played in a number of their tournaments over the past few days, getting very deep in a few, but not cashing in any. I was disappointed I didn't fare better, but truly enjoyed every minute of it. It felt so good to be back on the felt in my element. I plan to play a lot more poker this Winter and have my best year yet in 2015. Unfortunately, I'm still not feeling great and continue to take the pain meds for my very sore throat. The nasty phlegm drip is still present, too. And, it looks like I'll need to use the feeding tube for at least a couple more weeks until I can swallow liquids and food without pain. Slowly, but surely, I know the healing process will occur. I just can't wait to function normally again.

TO BE CONTINUED....

Friends' Comments...

Scott G.
Keep up the fight my friend. You are a winner and we love ya!

John H.

I hope you "listen" to your body and take things slowly. Don't jump back into poker quite so fast. You've been through quite an ordeal. xoxo

Duane M.

Carpe Diem!

Chapter 49

HALLOWEEN, DOUGLAS STYLE

Oct 25-26

HERE IN OUR SMALL COMMUNITY of Douglas, MI (pop. 1,200) we celebrate Halloween in a big way! Each year, at 10pm on the Saturday before Halloween, we have the Douglas Adult Walking Parade on Center St in downtown Douglas. It's called "Adult" for a reason, as it's more "R" rated than PG13. I don't really recommend it for the kids unless you want to answer a lot of questions!

For the past three years at Zing, we've hosted the parade pre-party and always have live music with Christy G & Velvet. We encourage our guests to come dressed in costume. About half do just that. This past Saturday night we had 110 folks join us for our four-course Halloween dinner. Our staff costume theme was "Night of the Living Dead", so I transformed myself, with the help of my friend, Lissa, into Zombie Rocker Girl. It was a fun, easy costume that showed off my now 22 lb weight loss and nicely covered up my feeding tube.

I didn't work on Friday night, so I had some decent energy on Saturday night and was also able to work, walk in the parade, and attend the after-party at The Dunes until about 11:30pm. Chris came into town for the weekend festivities and Elizabeth also met up with us at The Dunes for some celebrating. I was in bed by 12:30am after scrubbing off all of my makeup and nail polish. Unfortunately, I was so exhausted that I slept through church and didn't get up until 11:30am.

Chris and I did some shopping in Saugatuck on Sunday afternoon and then went to Bingo at The Dunes for a couple of hours. Neither of us were winners, but we had a winning weekend! It felt so good to be out and about for a bit. I have a long way to go in feeling better and getting back to normal, but I'll get there. Right now, it's one day at a time and I'm looking forward to a little improvement each day.

TO BE CONTINUED....

Friends' Comments:

Charlene P.
Your Facebook pic was great and I was happy to see your smiling faces. Take care and get the rest you need to get back to good health. Small steps, not giant leaps!

Duane M.
You two looked fabulous! It was a fun parade and a great turn out. So great seeing you there. Plus, we couldn't complain about the weather. Kudos.

Chapter 50

Finally Starting to Feel Better

Oct 28

I've been sleeping a lot better lately, not waking up every hour with a coughing attack from my phlegm drip or needing to spit out a mouthful of saliva. After a good nine hours of sleep last night, I got up feeling better than usual. I did my hour-long feeding, showered, dressed, folded laundry, checked emails and went to work for a few hours. My throat didn't hurt quite as much as it usually does and I was able to swallow my saliva more often than I have been. These are good signs and hopefully each day I'll be seeing some improvement.

I had a check-in appointment today with Dr. Zachem, my chemo doctor. I weighed in at 206 lbs, so I'm down about 24 lbs from when I started treatments. No one is concerned yet, as long as I don't continue to lose more weight. I should be stabilizing, or even gaining a little weight, moving forward in the healing process. Dr. Zachem was very pleased to tell me that he did not feel any unusual lymph nodes and thinks the chemo and radiation treatments together "got them." I still need to wait three months for everything to heal before I can be tested, but this news is very encouraging.

I finished my day with an afternoon meeting at Eiizabeth's to discuss Business Association projects. We got a lot done and I'm feeling good about all of the progress being made. So overall, it was a really great day!

TO BE CONTINUED....

Friends' Comments:

Doug G.
You will be in fabulous shape for the cruise!

Cheryl C.
Things are looking up. All good!!

Scott G.
Great news, Jim! Keep up the good work.

Chapter 51

I Feel Human Again!

Oct 31

IT'S HALLOWEEN! I FINISHED MY radiation treatments 11 days ago and today I finally feel human again. I think I've been walking around in a chemo/radiation coma for the past two months… until now. It feels so good to be heading toward "normal". I have a long way to go, but I can definitely see improvement. It's a one day at a time kind of thing. I worked in the office for five hours, took an hour nap, and was on the floor in the restaurant tonight for three hours. We had a nice bar crowd and I enjoyed mingling and catching up with folks. People said that my "color had come back" and that I "looked a lot better than the last time they saw me." I liked those comments. Clearly, my seven weeks of cancer treatments really kicked my butt. I'm not sure how I got through it all, but I did. It's nice to be on the mend. The worst is over.

TO BE CONTINUED….

Friends' Comments:

Donald M.
Celebrate each new day as you begin to realize the real meaning of "normal."

Kristin A.

SO glad to hear you feel like you're turning a corner! You are such a strong person, Jim, and you have an amazing support system. Keep walking forward -- big, positive movements daily!

BJM

Welcome back!

Janie F.

Cheers to "normal!" Admire your strength, Jim.

Chapter 52

What Is My Legacy?

Nov 1-2

Last night at Zing was awesome! We had a small, but very intimate, crowd in the martini lounge with many guests that I really enjoy. Their concern for my health and well-being was overwhelming. Everyone was checking in with me to see how I was doing. It felt so good to catch up with folks and let them know that I'm feeling human again. I got through the entire evening without getting nauseous or really tired...a first! I think I'm back in action.

We turned the clocks back an hour last night, so it felt good to get some extra sleep. I woke up this morning excited to go to church because I've missed the past two Sundays. I thought that Elizabeth might like to join me, as she is not currently a member of any church in the area and mentioned that she'd like to start attending again. I sent her a text and she replied that she'd love to go.

I was struck today by both the Call to Worship and Pastor Sal's homily. The Call to Worship was: "Those who cared for, nurtured and protected us, those who have loved us unselfishly, those who have inspired us to greater things, those who have listened to us when we're struggling, those who shared their wisdom with us and enabled us to see more of the truth...They are always with us."

I couldn't help but think about my parents, and a few coaches, teachers, trainers, close friends and loved ones, who have been so influential during different stages of my life. Together they have helped shape who I am, what I believe and how I approach things. But more importantly, they instilled the confidence in me that I could accomplish anything, if I really wanted to. I feel so blessed that I've been touched in this way. I've been a fighter my whole life. Nothing has been given to me on a silver platter. I've had to earn what I have and fight for what I want. This fighter trait certainly helped me get through my cancer treatments. I wanted to quit, but I didn't. "Quit" is a word that just doesn't exist in my vocabulary and I'm thankful for that.

Pastor Sal's homily today was "What's Your Legacy?" He challenged us to think about what it is that we want to leave behind and be remembered for when we pass. Interestingly, most people are remembered for what they've done for others, not for what they did for themselves. To have a meaningful legacy, it appears that one must be unselfish and have made a real difference in someone else's life or a group of peoples' lives. This could take many forms from monetary support and contributions to emotional and/or inspirational influence and impact. I definitely need to give more thought about what I want my legacy to be and work harder to make that a reality.

TO BE CONTINUED....

Friends' Comments:

Donald M.
Thanks for sharing your thinking. If we all followed a couple of simple thoughts like "doing the right thing" and "treating people right", there would be an outbreak of contagious smiles.

Marilyn B.
Wow...lots to consider. Thanks for sharing this...and your thoughts, Jim. Glad you are feeling human again.

Elizabeth B.

Loved the service. Thanks for including me. Pastor Sal's words ring so true, especially the unselfish giving without expectation of reward. We are entering one of my favorite times of year. It's all about the giving, not what we get in return! To be of service to others is the greatest blessing of all! Jim, your spiritual and emotional growth through this journey has been miraculous to behold. Thank you for letting me be a part of it. Love you, xoxo

Chapter 53

I'm on the Mend!

Nov 4

FOR TWO MONTHS, DURING AND immediately after my treatments, I felt like a walking zombie in a coma state. Imagine living 24/7 with both the worst case of tonsillitis ever and a horrific flu that never goes away. You can't eat, drink, swallow, or barely talk. You're so tired all the time that all you want to do is curl up in a ball on the couch and sleep. This was my life from Sept 9-Oct 28, but things are changing now!

I'm excited to say that I'm officially on the mend. I've had a great few days and am feeling so much better. My sore throat is improving a bit each day and my nasty post-nasal phlegm drip is almost gone. I'm not collecting saliva in my mouth and spitting it out in a cup anymore. I have a renewed energy and am more motivated to get out and do things. I don't get nauseous when I smell different aromas. And, most exciting of all is that I've actually been able to eat small portions of real food, some tapioca pudding the other night and a half-cup of chicken pasta soup last night.

My taste buds are still a mess, but I think they might be starting to return. For the past few weeks when I tried to eat real food, it was like wet paper and I had to spit it out. Sweets do not sit well with me at all. The pudding I had the other night didn't taste right, but I was able to swallow it and the coolness felt good on my throat. Interestingly, I did start to taste the chicken pasta soup I had last night and I liked it. I had to really chew up the pasta bow ties, veggies, and chicken pieces to get them down my inflamed throat, but I was successful. As funny as it sounds, this is a big accomplishment since I haven't eaten real food in over ten weeks. I'm scheduled to have my feeding tube removed on November 21, but need to prove to my docs and myself that I can maintain my weight through normal eating. So, I'm on my way. I'm starting to feel so much better and human-like again. It's a huge relief!

TO BE CONTINUED....

Friends' Comments:

Brian C.
Great news, Jim!! I'm sure that Bombay Sapphire will also taste good to you soon!

Faye C.
So glad you are getting back to your old self. Baby steps, Jim. You are doing FABULOUS!

Duane M.
Good to hear, Jim. It's all up hill from here to a full recovery. Priceless!

Chapter 54

A Different Perspective on Things

Nov 6

I had a meeting early this morning with Rose, a sales rep from a local newspaper. We haven't been in touch since late Spring, so she wasn't aware of my battle with cancer. Rose asked me how I was doing, so I told her that I was on the mend and starting to feel a little better. We got into a discussion about cancer and how it can turn your life upside down. Rose asked me "how I've changed" as a result of having to deal with this hurdle. I sat for thirty seconds or so and really thought about her question.

I realized I am different now in a number of ways. At the top of the list is that I have re-discovered my spirituality. I've never been very religious, but have always felt some kind of connection to a higher power. During my cancer bout, I've found myself continually reaching out to that higher power. In return, I've been given the strength and belief that I can overcome this temporary obstacle that has been placed in front of me. I also found church again and have become a member of Douglas United Church of Christ. I feel at home there and am re-energized when I attend Sunday service.

The second way I've changed is that I have much less tolerance for insignificant, petty issues. Clearly, we all have issues that we're faced with every day. Whether it's work, friend, partner, family, or socially-related, they are present and have an influence on how we think, act and live our life. On a personal level, we tend to obsess over the smallest issue and feel the need to draw others in to vent, get perspective, or generate empathy.

However, what I've now learned from my experience is that there is no bigger issue than facing a life-threatening illness, like cancer.

When you are looking at no guarantee of being cured and possibly dying, everything else pales in comparison. When you feel physically sick 24/7 for ten weeks, can barely muster up the strength to get out of bed or off the couch, and just want to hide in the dark, curl up and cry from the pain, nothing else really matters. I will not let non-critical, insignificant, or inane issues take precedent, whether they are self-generated or those of a friend or an acquaintance. They are not worth the time or energy to worry about because honestly, in the larger scheme of things, they are not life-changing and, ultimately, will work themselves out. As a result of this learning, I believe I have more clarity around what is and isn't important in life which, in turn, has mellowed me out a bit. It feels good.

Another way I've changed is that I have a renewed faith in the genuine goodness of people. I continue to be overwhelmed (in a great way) by the caring outreach and support I've received from my friends, local community, restaurant guests, acquaintances, high school buddies I haven't seen in years, and my four angels (Chris, Elizabeth, Scott and Dr. Julie.) I've received so many cards, calls, gifts, and flowers. Most importantly, it has been the heartfelt conversations I've had with so many of you who have checked in on me to see how I'm doing. Knowing that you all truly care has made a huge difference and helped me to maintain a positive attitude through this horrific ordeal.

Lastly, something that has been reinforced for me over the past few months is how important it is to live life to its fullest every day. Don't wait. Do it now... while you are healthy and can! Fortunately, I've always lived this way. I have a "work hard, play hard" philosophy and have been blessed to have already experienced a very full life in my 54+ years. I've done almost everything I want to do and have very few things left on my "To Do" list. I'm certainly not ready to "check out", but if I were to die tomorrow I know that I've lived my life to the fullest and would absolutely have no regrets. So don't wait to do the things you really want to do. Figure out a way to do some of them now, because there may not be a tomorrow. Thank you, Rose, for asking me today "how I've changed." I do have a different perspective on things now.

TO BE CONTINUED....

Friends' Comments:

Lauren F.

Words of wisdom, Jim, words to live by. My brother once told me that his life-threatening illness was his greatest gift because it taught him what's really important in life and he was able to live it fully. We are in your corner! Coming by tonight. xoox

Donald M.

Jim, Ally and I could not agree more with your perspective. Living life to the fullest each day is often lost in the moment to moment, day to day challenges. Everyone needs to change their perspective to clearly see what is important in life. The next time someone cuts you off while driving just think, "Wow! they must really have a bad case of diarrhea... hope they make it." It puts a smile on your face and relieves the tendency to get upset! It is all about perspective.

Duane M.

You have changed for the better. The top priority is now in line with life. God has a way of making us all take a step back and reassess what's important. You are a good man and have touched a lot of people in your life lesson. Proud of you and we continue our prayers for your full recovery. D&J

Chapter 55

VEGAS Baby!

Nov 8-9

IN ORDER TO HELP ME get through my treatments, I set some goals for myself. First, I wanted to be healed enough to go on a Caribbean cruise on November 30th with my friend, Zing manager, and angel, Scott...and, more importantly, without my feeding tube. Second, I really hoped to be in Vegas the week of November 7 (just three weeks after treatments ended) to play in the Venetian DeepStack, Heartland Poker Tour, and World Series of Poker Circuit events.

GOOD NEWS! I'm in Vegas now at the Rio All Suites hotel writing this journal entry. I flew out on Saturday afternoon and arrived at the Rio after doing some critical "food"shopping. Unfortunately, my throat is still too sore to eat much, so my primary source for eating and drinking is my best friend, Mr. Feeding Tube. I found a grocery store in a shopping center near the Rio and purchased four six-packs of Boost high protein drink. Each has 240 calories. Since I didn't want to pack or ship my Jevity, this seemed to be the best option. I will be consuming a six-pack per day plus trying to eat soup, which seems to be the only thing my taste buds and throat will accommodate. It seems like my "salty" taste buds are just starting to have a reawakening. I ate an 8 ounce cup of chicken noodle soup yesterday while playing poker. This was huge for me! It's the first significant food I've had in ten weeks. It felt really good to get it all down without too much of a problem.

Sadly, my "sweet" taste buds are missing in action. Ice cream, pudding, milk shakes, smoothies are not interesting to me and do not taste good right now. Ice coffee black, however, has become a viable option, so I'm excited about that. I've really missed my coffee. Hopefully, I'll make good progress in expanding my food and drink options over the next few days. I still haven't had any alcohol in over three months and, honestly, I don't miss it at all. It doesn't taste good either. My docs tell me that my taste buds may take up to three months to come back and, when they do, they likely will be different than before. Things I used to like might not be popular with me anymore and things I didn't enjoy might actually be appealing. Go figure.

Yesterday, I played in the Seniors Event $400 No Limit Holdem (NLH) at the Venetian DeepStack. If you're over 50 (I'm 54) in poker, you're a Senior. Sadly, I was knocked out early in Level 3 by a very aggressive, crazy guy who made a ridiculous call on my All In on the turn and hit his three outer on the river. ARGH. It happens. So, I went over to Aria and played in their NLH event and placed 16th of 149 players. I won $160 for my $135 entry and netted $25. LOL. At least I cashed. Las Vegas is a happy place for me! I love the game of poker and have really honed my skills over the past few years to become quite competitive. I've done well in 2014 and plan to have a big 2015. It's Vegas, baby!

TO BE CONTINUED....

Friends' Comments:

Paula H.
Keep the good news coming! Wonderful that you are hitting these fun goals now.

Scott G.
You've won already. Now kick some butt! Congrats.

Chapter 56

WHAT A DIFFERENCE A WEEK MAKES

Nov 16

IT HAS BEEN ALMOST A week since I last made a journal entry. I've had a great time here in Vegas, although haven't been too successful at the poker tables this trip. I still have a few days left, so hopefully my luck will change. I'm excited to report that I'm now eating more regularly and no longer depending on the feeding tube. It seems like my taste buds are slowly returning, so I'm really optimistic. What works best for me are soft foods, as they are much easier to swallow. Cream-based soups, soft bread & butter, angel hair pasta carbonara, penne alfredo, eggs benedict on a croissant, and scrambled eggs are the big winners so far. Disappointingly, anything that has peppery or hot spice in it, burns my throat and sets it on fire. I used to put pepper and Tabasco sauce on everything, so this is an adjustment. I feel like I've lost another five pounds while I've been out here, but now that I can almost eat a full meal my weight should start coming back. I'm concerned that my docs at The Cancer Center won't be happy with the additional weight lost when I see them on Friday to get my tube out, but I've been trying not to rely on Boost and have instead been forcing myself to eat. I do think, however, that they'll be really pleased with how quickly I've shown progress in healing. We'll see.

The good news is that I know I'll be able to handle eating on the cruise without a problem. Scott and I leave on Thanksgiving Day for Fort Lauderdale and will be there a few days before heading into the Caribbean aboard the Celebrity Silhouette. I hear its snowy and quite cold back home in Michigan, but even Las Vegas was a cool 47 degrees this morning when I got in my car. The high will be 58 and is perfect for today's Las Vegas marathon, which I will be running in my mind. Time to hit the poker room.

TO BE CONTINUED....

Friends' Comments:

Lauren F.
You're winning the life marathon! Your luck has changed. Poker will eventually follow. So happy for you dear. Xo

Cory R.
Hi Jim, such a great report. I am so happy to hear you are finally able to eat some things. I remember how you'd douse your eggs with pepper and Tabasco! Have a fun in Vegas and good luck!

Chapter 57

ALMOST FEELING LIKE "ME" AGAIN

Nov 23

I GOT BACK FROM MY 11-day trip to Vegas on Thursday evening. I'm really glad I went. I needed to get out of my condo and do something I really like. I was feeling a bit "closed in" after being captive during my treatments. I had a pretty good poker run making two final tables and placing 4th and 5th in those tourneys. This has been my best poker year ever and I feel like I'm going to win big in 2015.

I finally started eating real food a week ago. As odd as it sounds, it's very hard work and quite a chore. My head immediately starts to sweat, as I sit down to eat in anticipation of how hard it's going to be to swallow. The sweating continues as I eat. My throat is still very sore, but not like it was, and my throat passage remains quite narrow due to swelling from the radiation. I can only handle soft foods like eggs, mashed potatoes, pastas, soups, mac & cheese, and bread (without crust). About 30 to 35% of my taste buds have returned, so right now my preference is for salty foods. Sweet items still sadly taste horrible and I can't handle any spicy foods or imbibe carbonated or alcoholic beverages because they all set my throat on fire. Hopefully, this will change soon before I board the Celebrity Silhouette for a 7-day Caribbean cruise next Sunday with Scott.

This past Friday, I had my check in appointments with both my radiation and chemo doctors. Elizabeth accompanied me for old time's sake as she wanted to thank the staff and docs for taking such good care of me during my seven weeks of treatments. They really were quite amazing!

Both Dr. Julie and Dr. Zachem were pleasantly surprised at how well I've done post-treatments and couldn't believe that I went to Vegas just 19 days after my last treatment. I told them that I still wasn't feeling great at that point, but that I thought I'd feel better playing at the poker tables, then hibernating another two weeks in my condo. I was right.

Dr. Julie also confessed that she didn't think I'd be able to eat this quickly or have my feeding tube out before the cruise. We talked about how having an end goal and positive attitude during treatments makes a huge difference in recovery, too. We also agreed that getting the feeding tube inserted at the end of week three of treatments, before I got really sick, was a very smart move. It kept me nourished and hydrated earlier in the process, and prevented me from losing even more than the 30 pounds I did lose. The four hours of feeding a day definitely wasn't fun, but it paid off in the end. I would highly recommend the feeding tube to anyone going through neck or throat cancer treatments. It made all the difference in the world for me! I've gained back about five pounds since October 20 and I have about fifteen more to go. It will come. I also need to get to the gym to get muscle definition back in my arms, shoulders and back. I feel a bit emaciated and lost a lot of muscle tone. The good news is that I lost a bit of weight in the abdominal region, so I almost have a flat stomach.

I can't tell you how good it feels to be functioning like a semi-normal human being again. As I look back to the evenings I tried to work at Zing, I realize that even though I was physically there, I wasn't really there at all. I think I was walking around in a drug-induced, coma state, going through the motions but not really being present. I tried my best, but I was just too sick. This past weekend at work felt good! I almost feel like "me" again. I've been waiting patiently for "me" to return and I know now that I'm so close to being fully back in action.

TO BE CONTINUED....

Friends' Comments:

Charlene P.

Wonderful news, Jim! Enjoy the cruise and have a Happy Thanksgiving!

Suzanne O.

Jim, it was great to see you back in your element during the Vegas trip. You mentioned "being present." Yup, these experiences remind us that we have a tendency to spend too much time not being present. Have fun on the cruise!

Star & Charlie

So very proud of you, Jim. You are a true inspiration! Love you very much.

Chapter 58

A Lot to be Thankful For

Nov 26

It's Thanksgiving Eve and I've been doing some reflecting that I want to share. Although the past few months have been really tough for me, I do have so much to be thankful for.

First, I'm thankful for all of the advances that have been made in cancer treatment technology. I can't imagine having cancer 10 or 15 years ago and getting the same kind of treatment and care I just recently received. I was so impressed by the chemo/radiation program I was put through (although it knocked me on my ass) and how thorough my doctors and caretakers were in tracking my progress.

This leads to the second thing I'm thankful for and that is EVERY-ONE on the medical teams at The Cancer Center who treated and took care of me during my seven weeks of treatments. I always felt like a person and never like a number.

Third, I'm so thankful for my friends and angels who have been by my side the entire time... from when I got the official cancer diagnosis on August 5 to when I completed my treatments on October 20 to the past four weeks of my healing and recovery process. Specifically, words cannot express how thankful I am for Elizabeth, Scott, Chris, and Dr. Julie who were always there for me even during my worst moments (and there were quite a few). Without them, I don't think I could have endured this.

Fourth, I'm so grateful for all of you who kept me in your prayers, sent me cards and gifts, responded to my journal entries here on CaringBridge or on Facebook, and checked in on me during the past four months. You have no idea how it kept my spirits up and encouraged me to keep going. There were so many times when I just wanted to curl up in a ball on my couch, draw all of the shades, and literally check out. But knowing you were out there rooting for me to beat this dreadful disease made all the difference.

Fifth, I'm so happy that I re-ignited the spirituality that was already within me. I had so much alone time to think, reflect and read. I started going to church, got so much out of it, and joined the Douglas Congregational UCC. I feel like I have a different outlook on things and clearly recognize what's important and not so important in life.

Finally, I'm thankful for my family, who I know has been so concerned about me.

Of course, there are so many other things to be thankful for, but I wanted to highlight these as they are most top of mind for me right now. Thanks again to all of you who continue to read my journal entries and send good thoughts and wishes. Please take a moment on this Thanksgiving Eve (or Thanksgiving Day) to reflect on what you're thankful for, too!

TO BE CONTINUED....

Friends' Comments:

Chris F.

I'm so thankful we met. You have taught me about courage, grace at life's toughest moments, and acceptance. Xoxoxo

Jessica C.

I am very thankful and blessed to have had the opportunity to help you through your cancer journey! You did awesome--so strong and courageous in the battle you fought! Was so good to see you last week and to hear that you are starting to feel better and more like yourself again! :)

Steven R.
I'm betting the "over" on 215 lbs after the cruise. Have fun, you deserve it!

Charlene P.
Will keep you in my thoughts and prayers until you beat cancer's butt. Enjoy your cruise and have a Happy Thanksgiving! Excellent words of wisdom and gratitude that made me thankful for good health and awesome friends.

Kathy D.
Very well said, Jim. Tough times really help you see what and who are important to you. May God bless you and keep you on the journey to good health.

Chapter 59

I'm Back (On Track)!

Dec 12

It has been 2 1/2 weeks since I last posted a journal entry. On Thanksgiving Day, Scott (my friend, angel and Zing manager) and I flew to Fort Lauderdale for our cruise on the Celebrity Silhouette to Cozumel, Grand Cayman, Jamaica and Labadee (a Royal Caribbean private island off the coast of Haiti). This was a gift I gave to Scott for his 50th Birthday back in June before my battle with neck cancer started.

Interestingly, going on this cruise became my goal to help me get through and recover from my chemo and radiation treatments. It worked. It felt so good to get on that ship, feel the ocean breeze, and kick back and relax for 8 days/7 nights. I got lots of rest. The ship was very nice. Entertainment was great. The ports were good, but the food was really bad...especially what I could taste of it.

My taste buds are only 40% recovered. I can taste "salty", but not sweet...except for vanilla. Chocolate tastes awful, which is a problem because it's my favorite. Hopefully, that taste bud will come back soon. Anything with citrus in it stings my throat and doesn't go down well. Unfortunately, I wasn't able to drink alcohol on the cruise because it also burns my throat and is just an unpleasant experience. As for food, I'm able to eat pastas with cream/marinara/meat sauces, lasagna, soft breads, butter, oatmeal, bananas, hot dogs, cheeses, salads, chicken, eggs, bacon/sausage/ham, turkey and gravy, mashed potatoes, soft hash browns, vanilla/tapioca pudding and soups. I'll be quite excited when beef tastes good again and I can indulge in a steak or a medium rare bacon cheeseburger on a pretzel roll with fries.

Unfortunately, I LOST five pounds on the cruise! Who does that? I'm down to 195 lbs from 230 lbs when I started my treatments..a 35 lb weight loss that my docs won't be happy about. Additionally, I'm a bit fatigued, always cold, have dry mouth often and get dizzy spells when I stand up after sitting. I spoke with Dr. Julie's assistant, Ronda, about this and it sounds like I'm dehydrated and need more protein and extra calories in my diet because my body is still healing. I'm working hard at eating three meals a day and supplementing them with Boost or Ensure as an in between meal snack.

Overall, I'm really feeling quite good and am back on track to better health and feeling normal. Each day my sore throat is improving to where I've stopped taking my morphine pain pill. The worst is definitely over. My PET Scan is now scheduled for January 16, when my throat should be completely healed. On Januaray 23, I will get the test results and am looking forward to hearing the words from Dr. Julie, "We got it. You are now Cancer-Free!" That would be the best Christmas gift ever.

TO BE CONTINUED....

Friends' Comments:

Cheryl C.
So glad you got away and enjoyed yourself. Keep on keepin' the faith.

Donald M.
Thanks for keeping us posted. We are so happy to hear your trip was a success. Your words are uplifting and encouraging for all of us. Without a doubt, the best words will be "WE GOT IT." Embrace the true meaning of Christmas throughout the holidays!

Chapter 60

Joy to The World

Dec 14

I WENT TO CHURCH ALONE this morning. It's the third Sunday of Advent and today's theme was "Joy". I was very moved by our Call to Worship:

Pastor: Joy to the world! But what is joy? Is it colorful? Is it expensive? Can it be gift-wrapped?

All: No, it's none of these.

Pastor: Is it happiness? Is it excitement? Is it blessedness?

All: Yes, it is these and more, much more.

Pastor: Joy is for now. It is completeness. It is consummation. It is holy.

All: Joy is that painting...on that day, at that time, in that place. Joy is that poem the umpteenth time through. Joy is that smile exchanged that day.

Pastor: And joy is the story of a baby, and wise ones, and angels, and shepherds, and stars.

All: It is not fact. It cannot be proved. But it is truth.

Pastor: In that story is completeness and consummation.

All: Because, in that life was completeness, and consummation, and holiness. Joy to the world!

The third candle in the advent wreath is pink. It is uniquely different from the other candles that are a bluish purple in color. It represents Joy. For me, joy usually comes in an unexpected moment. It is a state of being that happens in the present and we need to be mindfully aware, so as not to miss it. There are small and sometimes larger moments of joy in each and every day. We need to recognize, feel and embrace them as they happen. There is nothing like joy. It feels so good when we have it in our lives.

As I progress through my recovery, I am joyfully grateful for the daily improvements in how I feel. Even with my cancer setback, I have so much to be joyful for in my life. I will test clean and cancer-free in January. A good test result will be pure joy, and a great relief. Rejoice always!

TO BE CONTINUED....

Friends' Comments:

Kathy D.
Joy is the little things in life that make you feel good. When you go through a traumatic event lots of " things" don't matter anymore. It becomes about the little things like nature, a sunset, a shooting star, a flower in bloom, a child's laugh, or a warm hand on your leg. It's the simple things! Wishing you joy and peace.

Donald M.
I read that happiness often depends on outside influence, while joy is the foundation of inward peace. The bible uses the word joy or rejoice over 300 times. It stands to reason if a person wants to embrace and feel true joy, they need to examine their own religious thinking. Jim, it sounds like you are absorbing a lot of joy in your life.

Kristin A.
JOY indeed! And rejoicing with you, Jim. Thank you for this wonderful reminder of what we should fill each and every day with.

Mary Kay B.
Thank you for sharing this beautiful call to worship! "It cannot be proved, but it IS truth!" Love it.

Chapter 61

Believe in the Wonders of Tomorrow

Dec 20

It has been a week since I last made a journal entry. No doubt you have been busy with Christmas shopping, wrapping presents, decorating the house, and baking Christmas cookies. I had three highlights this week I'd like to share.

First, Elizabeth had Chris and me to her home for dinner on Wednesday evening. The fireplace emitted a glowing warmth, the cats searched for cozy places to snuggle up, the table was set beautifully, and Christmas was in the air. Elizabeth made her popular shrimp newburgh and served it on rice. Perfect for me. It was easy to eat and I enjoyed the flavorful cream sauce. She also baked Pillsbury crescent rolls (my favorites) and made a salad.

Chris and I had such a nice time. The Holidays are really about being with people you care about who care about you, right? I bought Elizabeth a few gifts as a "thank you" for everything she's done for me over the past few months. I don't think I could have gotten through my radiation and chemo treatments without her. She kept me positive and made me laugh, even when I didn't want to. Elizabeth and I have had many close personal conversations. One of the things we talk a lot about is living in the present and maximizing each day to its fullest, since you just don't know if you'll be around tomorrow.

We really can't control tomorrow, so why worry about it? You can, however, be mindfully aware of and fully engaged in your present. I've been trying very hard to live this way. It helped me take one day at a time during my treatments and kept me from thinking too far ahead about what I was going to be up against later with side effects, pain, weight loss, and overall discomfort.

One of my gifts to Elizabeth, was a 6' decorative wall hanging with pieces of a compelling phrase strung together. The top piece said, "BE-LIEVE". The next two pieces connected underneath it said, "IN" and "THE". They were followed by "WONDERS", "OF, and "TOMOR-ROW." Yes, "Believe in the Wonders of Tomorrow!" We don't know what they are yet. We can't control what they're going to be. But we can be hopeful that they're waiting for each of us in the future. I was so excited that Elizabeth loved the gift. It's already hanging prominently in her home.

Another highlight of my week was celebrating Christmas with Chris, which is also his Birthday. Given our schedules, we won't be together again until New Year's Eve, so it was great that we could spend some quiet, quality time with each other on Wednesday and Thursday. We saw the movie, "The Theory of Everything", and really enjoyed it. The performances by the lead actor and actress were amazing and both of them, along with the movie, have been nominated for Golden Globes.

Chris and I exchanged gifts on Thursday eve and finished planning our January vacation. He's never been on a cruise, so we found a last minute deal on a 6-night cruise from Fort Lauderdale to Key West, Cozumel, and Grand Cayman. We're really looking forward to it. Chris got me a Bluetooth speaker, so now I have music in my place that I can program and control with my iPhone. Ahhhh, the power of technology!

The final highlight of my week was at Zing last evening. It seemed like everyone who lives on Amity Lane was at Zing. The martini lounge was abuzz with laughter, song, conversation, drinks and eats. Everyone was so joyous. The festive spirit was contagious. It made me feel so good that everyone was enjoying themselves. I left with a big smile on my face.

In a few hours, Scott is taking me to the airport. I'm going to be spending most of next week with my Dad and Cheryl in Florida. I haven't seen them since my brother Ed's wedding in October of 2013. I'm really looking forward to our Holiday visit. It has been too long.

Don't forget to "Believe in the Wonders of Tomorrow" as you progress through the upcoming Holiday week. It's not always a happy time for folks, but it certainly is a magical time. Embrace it!

TO BE CONTINUED....

Friends' Comments:

Mary Kay B.
What a beautiful post. There is truly so much to celebrate this year. Thank you for sharing your journey with all of us. You are a true blessing. Merry Christmas!

Kathy D.
Merry Christmas! Wishing you a Happy New Year filled with good health and peace.

Chapter 62

FEELING SURPRISINGLY GOOD DURING THE HOLIDAYS!

Dec 21-29

I HAVE TO ADMIT THAT I'm not a big fan of the Holidays. Let me explain. While I was with my ex-partner for ten years, we had a "Walton-type" Christmas with his family in Ohio. I always looked forward to seeing his brothers, nieces, nephews, aunts, uncles, and parents, while they were still with us. It was a joyous time full of laughter, fun, food, drink, celebration and 20-plus people...just what I always thought Christmas should be like.

When Matt and I split up a couple of years ago, Christmas became a lonely time of year for me, as it is for many. It's hard to get excited when you're constantly being bombarded by tv commercials showing "happy family" Holiday get-togethers and Today Show segments featuring what to make for your big Christmas party or Holiday dinner. This is especially difficult when your family is very small, older, separated by distance, and/ or lacking children. So last year, I decided to go to Vegas (one of my happy places) for Christmas and play poker. I had a great time, but it didn't feel like Christmas.

This year, I went to see my 82 year old Dad and Cheryl (stepmom) in Florida and combined it with a trip to Fort Lauderdale to see my friend, Nancy, and play some poker. I'm so glad I did. There was no Christmas tree or fancifully decorated home, but there was true joy in just being able to spend quality, "one-on-one" time with people that really matter and I know truly care about me. I think that's what's really important about the Holidays, along with remembering and being thankful for the birth of Christ.

It was reassuring for Dad & Cheryl to see me looking and feeling better, and in the past nine days I've moved from being 80% "back to normal" to about 90%. I have a lot more energy and am starting to develop a small appetite. Eating is no longer a chore and my taste buds are improving. I put on three pounds this week and am up from 190 to 193 lbs. It's nice to hear from folks that I'm looking healthier. I'd like to get back to 215 to 220 lbs, which is a much better weight for me.

Tomorrow is New Year's Eve. We'll have a full house at Zing and it will be a fun, high energy night. Chris will be joining me and I'm really looking forward to ringing in 2015 with him. I am feeling surprisingly good during these Holidays and am optimistically hopeful that I'll get the good news that I'm cancer-free in a few weeks.

TO BE CONTINUED....

Friends' Comments:

Charlene P.

I'll be praying for you and good news in January. The very best to you always and Happy New Year!

Elizabeth B.

Happy New Year, Darling! As I ring in 2015, I will reflect on our miraculous journey together and remain grateful for all you have taught us about faith, courage, and strength! You ARE my hero! Love you, XOXO

Chris F.

Brought tears to my eyes. Nice entry!

Chapter 63

IT'S A NEW YEAR FULL OF HOPE

Dec 30 - Jan 2

I DON'T KNOW ABOUT YOU, but I'm not a big fan of New Year resolutions. When I made them in the past, I usually scored an "incomplete" by the end of January. I do, however, think it's a positive step to take inventory on the past year and consider changes and new opportunities you'd like to explore in the new year. 2014 wasn't so good for me. I was diagnosed with depression early in the year and then battled neck cancer for the second half of the year. So I'm ready, very ready, to turn the page and start the new chapter of January, 2015.

My mantra for this new year is "Have Hope." I'm releasing myself to my higher power to help protect me, guide me in the right direction, support me in making good decisions, and mold me into a better man. I am so hopeful that 2015 will be a breakthrough year personally and professionally for me. While I was sick, I had a lot of time to think, soul search, and evaluate my past and present. But really it's about looking ahead, because you can't change what has happened. You can, however, influence what lies ahead. There is no doubt that the Big C has given me a life-threatening scare. I will beat it and know that I will be cancer-free in 2015. I will leverage this gift of new life to its absolute fullest each and every day because life is just too short to wait to live your dreams. We just don't know when our individual number will be called for heaven's gate, so we must take complete advantage of our life while we our blessed to have it and are in good health to enjoy it.

I really like the old saying, "Don't put off to tomorrow what you can do today." It's easy to find excuses that may prevent us from accomplishing this goal. But at the end of the day, tomorrow may not come. So we must seize each and every day at that moment. I believe that 2015 offers new Hope for all of us, but we must each make a concerted effort to embrace and move forward with those things we are hopeful for.

In closing, I'm saddened to let you know that Chris' dad died on New Year's Day. He was 81 and had been in assisted living and then hospice care for his last few days. Chris is managing quite well given the circumstances. Please keep him and his family in your thoughts and prayers.

TO BE CONTINUED....

Friends' Comments:

Donald M.

The New Year provides an opportunity for renewal and reconnection with the heart. If we all follow your example of being courageous and confident, 2015 will be the year to live our dreams. Chris is in our thoughts and prayers.

Jeanne S.

I agree that 2014 was very trying. I lost my sister in April to cancer and have been struggling ever since. I take your posts as a message to me personally. I agree with Every Single Thing you post. God bless you Jim, and Chris, and may 2015 be a great year for all of us!

Colleen R.

Thanks Jim, for your upbeat attitude toward life. We can all take a page from your journal and practice from it. My condolences to your partner for the loss of his father. Losing our loved ones is NOT easy. One of the most difficult experiences in our lives, as well as our own life-threatening experiences.

Chapter 64

It's a Bad Dream, Right?

Jan 4

I WOKE UP IN THE middle of the night with my heart beating fast and sweat dripping from my brow. I rarely remember dreams, but this one is vivid...and I have to say I'm just a little freaked out by it. Dr. Julie, my radiation oncologist and one of my angels, approached me at the entrance of The Cancer Center and asked me to walk with her. I had gone to Metro Health Hospital for my PET scan a week earlier and now the results were in. The look on Dr. Julie's face was alarming. She didn't want to make eye contact with me. I knew there was a problem. I said, "It didn't go away, did it?" Tears rolled down her face and she said, "No, I'm so sorry" and she hugged me. Dr. Julie told me that Bonnie, the radiologist, saw a "pea wrapped in an egg" and that the primary cancer spot had now moved 10% to the right. I was in disbelief and couldn't understand how this could be happening. And then I woke up.

Now I'm wondering what exactly this means? I've been so positive about kicking cancer's ass and being cured. I'm feeling really good right now and have made such great progress healing fairly quickly. Is this just a big tease? Am I being set up for a huge fall? Where did this ridiculous nightmare come from? Perhaps it's in my subconscious lingering because I've tried so hard not to think about losing the battle? I know I'm an expert at compartmentalization. Most likely I put my cancer in a box and placed it far back on its own shelf out of sight, mind, and reach. Is it trying to remind that it's still lurking there in the dark? It just can't be. It has to be gone. I don't even want to consider it as a possibility. The thought of having to go through more radiation and chemo treatments or surgery makes me sick. I wouldn't wish it upon my worst enemy. I just have to believe that this was my subconscious being disrupted somehow. I'm going to release this now and send it up. I will be cancer-free at the end of January. This is just a bad dream.

TO BE CONTINUED....

Friends' Comments:

James P.

We also are offering your positive thoughts and feelings up to the Lord. He will answer your wishes, as He is a healer. We are always with you Jim, and so is He. All our love, Dad and Cheryl

Brian C.

You are right to "Release it now and send it up", Jim. That's the best thing to do. Just a bad dream. You are kicking cancer's ass.

Donald M.

Remember your own words of living each day focusing on the positive! It was a bad dream! As they say in the song..."Let it go!" and enjoy the beauty of each day.

John T.

Sounds like the pea wrapped in an egg is a description of your compartmentalizing, not the cancer itself. As in all things, balance is the secret. Let your mind do its job and let your inner voice do its part, too. That is why you are still seeing the doctors AND going to church at the same time. They both have a place in your life.

Cheryl C.
Your brain is duking it out with your biggest fear. It is part of your journey, not an omen. Stay positive. You have all that is good on your side. Xoxo

Lauren F.
Dreams are often fears or worries being worked out by the subconscious. You don't have any reason to believe this right now, so great you let it go. Wishing you a peaceful day! xo

Chris F.
It's just a dream. I KNOW you are cancer-free!!

Chapter 65

Positive Poker Week, Nervous about PET Scan

Jan 15

I just returned from Durant, OK yesterday after spending a week there playing in the World Series of Poker Circuit Events at Choctaw Nation. I had a very good run placing 6th and final tabling one event, and then finishing 42nd of 4,053 players in a record-setting $365 No Limit Hold'em event, where I won almost $4,000. I've had an awesome late December through January and am playing my best poker in eight years.

I think 2015 is going to be my year and I plan to be more active than previous years. Poker is my passion. There is nothing like it. I can play for hours and it doesn't phase me one bit. I truly love the game! Tonight, I was invited to play in a local cash game with five other guys and I came home ahead $125. I hope I'm asked back.

Tomorrow morning, Elizabeth is picking me up at 9:30am to take me to Metro Health for my PET scan. This test will identify if I've kicked the cancer or if it's still lurking in my neck and throat region. I'm confident it's gone, but can't help thinking about the "What if it's not?" scenario. I'm not nervous about the process of getting the PET scan, but rather am anxious about receiving the results on January 27. I just have to be cancer-free. If I'm not, I don't know if I can go through another seven weeks of radiation and chemo, or the surgery option that was previously discussed with me. It will not be pretty. I'm really very optimistic that all is good, however it's hard to not think about the other side of things.

Friends' Comments:

Dominique L.

Jim, I have faith in you. I will send up positive prayers your way.

Dar W.

There is something powerful about one's intention. If you think it, believe it! It will be so. Prayer is also powerful. Good intentions and positive prayer being sent, Jim.

Edward P.

Positive thoughts give positive results. It will go well!

BJM

After what you have been through, it is So normal to have fear. Sending positive energy your way that you have firm cancer-free results. Here's a hug!

Kathy D.

Good luck, Jim. Sending prayers and positive vibes! Hoping you get great news, but also know that you are strong and CAN do whatever you need to do. Take one day at a time and one step at a time.

Chapter 66

SUPER CRUISE WITH CHRIS, BUT PET SCAN REALITY SETTING IN!

Jan 17-26

CHRIS AND I STARTED DATING in July, three weeks before I got diagnosed with cancer on August 5. I knew my treatments were going to make me really sick, so I told him that I'd understand if he didn't want to endure them with me. I gave him lots of outs, but he didn't take any of them. Chris was by my side the entire time whenever he could be. He was such a rock of support, one of my beautiful angels.

Since I started going downhill about two weeks into my treatments, Chris and I didn't have the opportunity to get to know each other while I was feeling well. Instead, he got to see me at my very worst as my daily radiation and weekly chemo consumed my body over a very difficult and unpleasant seven weeks. During this time, I tried each day to live in the moment just to get through it, but did set future goals to strive for. One of those was to take a vacation with Chris once I was feeling better. We decided on a Caribbean cruise departing out of Fort Lauderdale and visiting the ports of Key West, Cozumel and Grand Cayman. Chris had never been on a cruise before or on a vacation without his four children, so this would be an exciting new experience for him.

We flew to Fort Lauderdale, spent the night at our friend Ryan's condo, and boarded the Carnival Conquest on the evening of Sunday, January 18. We had an amazing six days on the cruise. Food, service, entertainment, and weather were all great. We also did quite well in the casino. But, most importantly, we got to spend quality time together with few external influences or interruptions. We really enjoyed ourselves and found that we travel well together. Upon returning from the cruise, we spent two additional days in Fort Lauderdale. Our vacation week flew by.

Before we knew, it we were landing at Gerald Ford International Airport in Grand Rapids, MI, while being greeted by 20 degree weather. Reality set in. Tomorrow I would be going to The Cancer Center to meet with Dr. Julie to get my PET scan results. I felt anxious and concerned. I'd been having nightmares during the past three evenings, waking up screaming, sweating, and breathing heavily. These were new occurrences. In the two I could recall, I was being attacked by strangers. In one with a gun in an antique collectibles store that I had just recently opened and in the other with a knife in a revolving office building door that I got stuck in when it stopped suddenly.

Why was I having these horrible dreams? Are the slightly dripping phlegm in the back of my throat, difficulty in swallowing, and raspy voice I have signs that the cancer isn't gone? I tried to pass it off, but it was difficult. Tomorrow the truth will be told.

TO BE CONTINUED....

Friends' Comments:

Chris F.
I had such an awesome vacation with you. Here's to more quality time enjoying each other!

Chapter 67

I'm Cancer-FREE!!!!!

Jan 27

THIS HAS TO BE ONE of the best days of my life. I'm officially Cancer-FREE! I beat the Big C! I'm a survivor!

Dr. Julie gave me and Elizabeth the incredible news I've been waiting to hear for almost six months. I don't have to go for more treatments. I don't have to endure surgery. The PET scan showed no "yellow glow" anywhere. Dr. Julie said it's the best PET scan I could have hoped for. There is no sign of any remaining cancer...anywhere. Words can't really describe how I'm feeling right now. "Relief" is probably the most accurate, followed by "Thankful."

I was so nervous driving to The Cancer Center with Elizabeth today. I had my Angel coin, from the nice local couple, and a tiny "Believe" fish that Elizabeth gave me in my jeans pocket. Rhonda weighed me in (200 lbs), took blood pressure (121/78) and checked oxygenation levels (100%), then updated my medical information. Deb, the nutritionist, came in to say "Hi" and check on me. I told her that I like my new weight. We laughed. Then Dr. Julie came in and gave us the "Thumbs up". I said softly, "It's gone?" She said, "Yes, it's gone." I exhaled and closed my eyes for a minute to process her words. It was a bit surreal. Elizabeth and I both got a bit teary. This nightmare was now over. The black cloud was lifted and the sun was shining through. I wasn't going to have to put up with any more pain or worry. Dying wasn't a possibility anymore. My life was renewed. I'm back.

I will continue to live in the moment and embrace life to its fullest each and every day! Thanks again for all of your thoughts, prayers, and support. You just can't know how much of a difference it has made for me. I feel so blessed to have you all in my lives. I plan to continue writing in this journal, when it makes sense to do so. I'm also going to explore getting it published. Perhaps it will help others who might be going through a similar experience and give them hope?! Cancer CAN be beaten! I'm proof of that now.

TO BE CONTINUED....

Friends' Comments:

Meg C.

Hi, Jim. You don't know me and I don't know you. My nephew Keith and his partner Jake told me about you when I found about my husband's diagnosis of metastatic squamous neck and throat cancer with occult primary. He was diagnosed last July. So, I suppose I stalked your progress through this site. I've rejoiced in your advances and have been eagerly waiting to hear about your progress regarding being able to eat, taste and swallow. I'm so happy that they have not found any more cancer cells, the little bastards. I know how difficult your journey has been. My husband still has a feeding tube that provides all of his nutrients and he's slowly learning how to swallow again. I wish you all the best and hope for many years of those cancer-free PET scans.

Steven R.

What a relief!

Arthur C.

This is so GREAT, Jim! I'm so happy for you. I just knew this is the way it would go. You did it! You're fabulous! I love you. WooHoo!!

Karen/Mike Z.

Answered prayers! Awesome news!!

Kathy D.

Happy Birthday...I know it's not your b'day, but it is the first day of the rest of your life! Live it to the fullest and enjoy. Make the best of the rest and have no regrets.

Lauren F.

I had tears in my eyes as I read your news. So happy for you. Live every moment to the full! xo

Annette C.

Fantastic. 90% was your incredible attitude and your zest for life!

Jeanne S.

What great news! Thank you for sharing your journey with us. Now... get living!

Debbie W.

Through my tears, I'm sending you a huge hug and heartfelt congratulations!

Duane M.

God has blessed a great man! So happy for the awesome news.

Charlene P.

OMG Jim, I honestly believe that this is the best news anyone could ever imagine. I am so happy and excited for you. My prayers have been answered and I'm so grateful. Glad you stayed strong and positive. I think this was because you had many people looking after you as well. Celebrate life, celebrate love and be happy.

Chapter 68

The Power Within You

Feb 4

I've had a week to reflect on my Cancer-FREE news. It feels amazing to know that I'm in the clear and don't have to endure surgery or more chemo and radiation. This past Sunday I went to church after a three week absence due to my travel and vacation schedule. It felt so good to be back. I feel spiritually lifted every time I enter church. Surprisingly, attendance was strong even with the cold, wintry weather and snowfall.

Ironically, Pastor Sal's homily was titled "One Power". He talked about how it's so easy for us to give up on our personal power if we let ourselves. For example, when someone makes you mad, you're letting them steal your power. When you think you can't do something or that you're not good enough to get the job you want, you're setting up your own false obstacles and barriers...another form of releasing your power.

Pastor Sal provided us with a definition One Power. It's OUR power. We need to harness it and let it work for us. It's the power within us that enables us to do things we never thought imaginable. I used my personal power to believe that I could battle and beat the Big C. It took so much out of me, but I did it. I wasn't going to let it take me down. I did not relinquish my power to the dreaded disease called cancer. I used my personal power and the positive energy from others to get me through four horrific months of pain and suffering. I did it, and am really proud of myself. At times, I didn't think it would be possible, but I kept tapping into my power within to persevere and win.

Jim Petzing

Do you believe in coincidences? I think they happen for a reason. When I first started attending Douglas UCC this past Fall, I met one-on-one with Pastor Sal so we could get to know each other better. He knew I was battling cancer and we talked a lot about prayer and believing that I would become cancer-free after my treatments. Pastor Sal gave me a book called "The Power Within" and asked me to read it. I did that during my recent poker trip to Oklahoma. I had been implementing many of the key concepts of that book already, but it was a great reinforcement.

As fate would have it, I planned to return that book to Pastor Sal this past Sunday, but left it on my kitchen counter. Then, lo and behold, his homily for the service was entitled "One Power" and focused on the power within each of us. I chatted with Pastor Sal after the service and told him this story and reminded him that he had given me the book. He told me to keep it and pass it on to someone I felt could benefit from it. Coincidence or not?

Try to maximize the power within you to the best of your ability each and every day. You'll see the difference it makes!

TO BE CONTINUED....

Friends' Comments:

Jan L.
Jim, thank you for turning me onto your cancer journey on Caring-Bridge. I love hearing your positive energy and ideas about how to live life to its fullest. I pray for your continued cancer free journey. I also absolutely love your restaurant so you have to stay healthy!

Dominique L.
I'm going to read that book. Thank you!

Duane M.

So happy for you! You are an inspiration to many. Kudos!

Kimberly L.

"One Power" can work for so many people for so many reasons. I am so happy that you found the power within yourself to keep strong and believe that you would beat the awful cancer that invaded your body. I hope you never have to endure that pain again.

Chapter 69

EMERGENCY LANDING AT O'HARE AIRPORT, NO FRONT LANDING GEAR

Mar 15

I CAN'T BELIEVE THIS HAPPENED today. I just lived through another one of my worst nightmares and likely one of yours. My elderly 81 year old mother lives in Connecticut and wasn't able to travel to Michigan to see me during my fight with the beast. It has been killing her, so I decided to fly out to visit her now that I had some time and was feeling so much better. You know how mothers worry. I wanted her to see for herself that I really was doing just fine, plus I was excited to spend her 82nd birthday with her on St. Patrick's Day, March 17.

So, I boarded United #2645, a small regional jet, for my first leg of the trip from Grand Rapids to Chicago O'Hare, where I would connect for my flight to Hartford, CT. On our approach to O'Hare, about five minutes from landing, the pilot informed us that his control panel did not show the successful deployment of the jet's front landing gear and that we would need to do a "fly by" air traffic control so they could take a look at the situation. Fifteen minutes later we were still flying over Lake Michigan and hadn't heard anything more from the pilot.

With over 5 million flyer miles under my belt, I knew we had a problem and that we were dumping fuel. Needless to say, I was getting quite concerned, at which point the pilot got back on the intercom system to inform us that, in fact, the front landing had not deployed and that we would be making an emergency landing. I could sense the tension in his voice, as could the other passengers. The pilot told us to listen carefully to our flight attendants and that he would do his absolute best to land us safely.

Shock and disbelief filled the cabin. At first there was total silence. My mind was racing in circles: "Are you kidding me?! I just beat cancer and now I'm going down in a plane crash. This can't be happening to me." Then, we all reached for our cell phones as the flight attendants were trying to get our attention to give us emergency landing instructions. Some people were calling their loved ones, while others were texting. I quickly texted Chris letting him know what was going on and providing him with my Mom's and Dad & Cheryl's phone numbers. I told him that if he didn't hear from me again to please let them know "I love them" and what had happened to me. I think he thought I was joking at first, but I cleared that up right away. I told him to pray. This was a news story in the making that I didn't want to be a part of.

Interestingly, I wasn't scared, but I was very anxious. I had come to terms with dying during my fight with cancer as that was a distinct possibility, but death no longer scared me. I had led such an amazing, blessed life! I was successful in my career, traveled to 90 countries across the world, owned two companies and a restaurant, had experienced some great personal relationships, and overcome many hardships... including beating cancer. However, I wasn't ready to go.

I knew my Higher Power was watching over me. I prayed hard for the pilot and a safe landing, while the flight attendants were instructing us how to brace ourselves properly for what was to be a very rough landing. I checked my position in the plane and liked my location. I was one row from the exit and in the middle of the plane. The woman in front of me was throwing up. A few people were crying. The flight attendants were now yelling "Brace, Brace, Brace, Brace" loudly as we were three minutes from "landing". It all was so surreal, in a bad way.

As we approached the Fed Ex runway at O'Hare, I tilted my head from the brace position to peak out the window as I knew we were about to touch ground. My heart was pounding. I saw the emergency vehicles racing after us down the runway. Were we going to flip, roll, crash, burn or explode? I closed my eyes. Suddenly, we were on the ground. It was a very turbulent, loud, shaky and scary landing, with a lot of scraping. I didn't see sparks or smell fire. Nothing was breaking or exploding around me. After about ten seconds, there was a fast braking of the jet and what seemed like a sharp left turn. The plane stopped. The pilot landed us safely! All 44 of us on board were shaken up, but okay. There didn't appear to be any injuries.

We all sort of sat there in shock for a moment and then we reached for our phones and began calling our loved ones to let them know we were safe. Chris always told me that if I saw a news story in the making, I should video it. So, I started doing that on my phone and did a narration of what had just happened to us all on United #2645. The pilot did an amazing job! He saved us. He was very pale with a relieved smile on his face. We all congratulated him at the front of the cabin, as we stumbled out of the plane on the stairs which were now parallel to the ground.

We were all put on a white school bus and asked to sign release forms indicating that we weren't injured. I took pictures of the plane and the emergency vehicles. I called Chris and texted my video and pictures to him. He asked if I would do a phone interview for his Grand Rapids ABC news station, which I did. Then I was barraged by Chicago news stations for the "story". My video and pictures of the event were shown on the evening news that night and on Good Morning America's Sunday show. It was "15 Minutes" of fame that I really didn't want.

We were given the option to continue on with our travel or rebook a flight for another day. I decided to continue on to Hartford as I really wanted to see Mom. That's what I was supposed to do and this "bump in the road" wasn't going to stop me.

Epilogue

FAST FORWARD. IT'S NOW JANUARY 23, 2017. I gained back all of the weight I lost, got my taste buds back, enjoy eating again, and feel great! I closed my restaurant, Zing, on October 31, 2015, after five years of long hours and much frustration. I just couldn't "crack the code" on how to make it profitable in the small seasonal resort town of Douglas, MI. It's still on the market and I'm hoping for a buyer any day now.

The good news is that I officially retired at the age of 55. So, I packed up and moved to Las Vegas, exactly one year ago today, to pursue my dream of becoming a full time professional poker player. Chris joined me and my two cats, Zing & Zang, on the 2065 mile drive from Douglas, MI. We've been together now for 2 1/2 years, but he still lives in Michigan with his four kids. We see each other once a month for a week or so. It's a long- distance relationship, but we're trying hard to make it work. He's still one of my angels.

I couldn't have asked for a better inaugural year of full time poker. I grossed over $225K in 2016 and was ranked 2nd in the USA and 3rd in the World for number of major tournament cashes with 50. I'm also writing a tournament poker column for Casino World Magazine and am hoping to pick up a sponsor or financial backer so I can play more higher end tournaments with the big boys!

As I think back to my battle with cancer, I can't help but feel so grateful for the life I'm blessed to live every day. I'm clearly one of the lucky ones and that's not forgotten on me. It's hard to believe how far I've come in such a short time...from a feeding tube to a successful poker career with many final tables in multiple poker tourneys. I've always been a fighter and know I can accomplish anything I set my mind to. I believe in ME!

Made in the USA
Columbia, SC
14 May 2017